Your
Gov't Your Rights

Simplifying the U S Constitution

By
W D May.

Your
Gov't Your Rights

Simplifying the U S Constitution

Table of Contents

Introduction

Imagine having a guide to the very foundation of our rights and freedoms—something that's so critical yet seems wrapped in complex legalese. That's exactly what we're diving into with every amendment of the U.S. Constitution, breaking it down into pieces so easy to understand, you'd think it's kid stuff. It's about taking these monumental laws that scaffold our daily lives and putting them into words that stick, whether you're just getting started with civic understanding or you've witnessed a dozen elections. This isn't just about dusting off an old document; it's about connecting dots from the past to our present and future. So, let's peel back the layers of history, examine the intricacies of rights, and, most importantly, bridge the gap between then and now. Through exploring each amendment, we're not only uncovering what's written between the lines but also why it matters to you, me, and everyone else walking the streets of this nation today.

Why Understanding Your Rights Matters

Imagine living in a world where the rules aren't clear. You could be playing a game, thinking you're scoring points, only to find out you've been playing it all wrong. That's a bit like navigating life without understanding your rights under the U.S. Constitution. It's the rule book that governs what the government can and cannot do, affecting everything from your privacy to your ability to speak freely. Knowing your rights isn't about getting a legal degree; it's about understanding the fundamentals of the game called democracy.

1

Knowing what's in the Constitution empowers you to stand up for yourself and others. Ever heard someone claim something was unconstitutional? Or maybe you've seen a law challenged in court on TV. These aren't just for judges and lawyers to decipher. When you understand the rights and freedoms guaranteed to you, you become better equipped to recognize when they're being infringed upon. It's like having a shield; you might not use it every day, but you'll be glad to have it when you need it.

But it's more than just self-protection. Understanding your rights is the first step in participating actively and responsibly in your community and country. Voting, protesting, or even having a heated discussion on social media about new laws—these aren't just acts of civic duty; they're exercises of your constitutional rights. And like any muscle, these rights become stronger and more resilient the more you use them. Knowledge here acts not just as power but as a vehicle for change, enabling you to contribute to the ongoing conversation about what justice and freedom should look like.

Then there's the less obvious, but equally important, aspect of empathy and understanding. By knowing the rights afforded to everyone, you're in a better position to appreciate the struggles others might face in their own experiences with rights violations. It bridges gaps, builds communities, and fosters a sense of shared guardianship over the freedoms so dearly fought for by generations past. It isn't just about knowing your rights in a narrow legal sense; it's about understanding how they apply to and unite us all in the pursuit of a more perfect union.

In a nutshell, understanding your rights matters because it transforms you from a passive observer to an active participant in the story of America. It makes you not just a beneficiary of the rights and liberties enshrined in the Constitution but a defender and promoter of them. And in today's world, where the pace of change is ever-accelerating, that understanding is more crucial than ever. It equips you with the knowledge to navigate the complexities of modern society, ensuring that as we move forward, we do so without leaving behind the principles that define us. So let's dive in, shall we? There's a lot to cover, and it all starts with a solid grasp of your rights.

A Brief History of the U.S. Constitution

The U.S. Constitution isn't just a piece of paper that's been lying around since the 18th century. It's a living, breathing promise of freedom, rights, and governance. How it came into existence is as fascinating as the document itself. So, let's take a walk back in time and see how this pivotal piece of American history came to be.

Before the Constitution, the newly independent states were bound by the Articles of Confederation, a document that left the national government so weak it couldn't even collect taxes. Imagine wanting to buy something but not having the money; that's how the government felt. Realizing this setup was a one-way trip to disaster, delegates from 12 of the 13 states (Rhode Island sat this one out) met in Philadelphia in the summer of 1787. Their goal was to create a stronger national government while still preserving the rights of the states.

The Constitutional Convention was no walk in the park. Picture a room full of some of the brightest minds of the era, and they're all trying to agree on what this new government should look like. It was a recipe for disagreement. Two plans battled it out: The Virginia Plan, which favored large states, and the New Jersey Plan, which protected the interests of smaller states. The result? The Great Compromise, offering a two-house Congress that satisfied both large and small states.

However, creating a blueprint for the government was only part of the battle. The issue of slavery was a massive elephant in the room. Northern and Southern states had deeply divided views on the matter. The Three-Fifths Compromise was their temporary fix, allowing a portion of the slave population to be counted for both taxation and representation purposes. It was a controversial decision, to say the least, and a stark reminder of the challenges the framers faced in creating a unified nation.

The final document also needed a mechanism for change, understanding that the future would bring challenges impossible to predict at the time. Enter the amendment process, a way to ensure the Constitution could evolve. The framers knew they hadn't created a perfect document, but they had created a flexible one.

After much debate and revision, 39 of the 42 delegates present on the final day signed the Constitution on September 17, 1787. It was a monumental moment, but now they faced an even bigger challenge: ratification. The Constitution required approval from nine states to become effective, and this sparked fierce debates across the country. Supporters of the Constitution, known as Federalists, clashed with opponents, the Anti-Federalists, who feared it gave too much power to the national government and lacked protections for individual rights.

The ratification process was a rollercoaster of persuasion, arguments, and compromises. Key states like Massachusetts, Virginia, and New York were battlegrounds for these debates. In some states, the promise to add a bill of rights was necessary to secure ratification. Finally, after New Hampshire became the ninth state to ratify in June 1788, the Constitution became the law of the land.

Yet, the story didn't end there. To fulfill the promises made during ratification fights, the first Congress added the Bill of Rights, ten amendments that explicitly protected freedoms like speech, religion, and the press, along with rights in criminal cases, such as the right to a fair trial. Ratified in 1791, these amendments are foundational to Americans' rights and freedoms.

So, from its precarious beginnings, the U.S. Constitution has endured as the framework of American government. Its creation was a complex blend of debate, compromise, and forward-thinking. It's more than a historical document; it's a testament to the resilience and flexibility of the ideals it enshrines.

Understanding the Constitution is crucial not just for historians but for every American. It shapes our laws, our politics, and our society. As we move forward, it's our guide and safeguard, ensuring that despite our differences, the promise of liberty, justice, and democracy endures for all.

Chapter 1:
The Structure of the Constitution

Imagine you've just gotten your hands on a map that tells you not only where you are but also outlines the rules of the road, ensuring you can navigate any journey safely. That's sort of what the U.S. Constitution is - a guidebook for navigating the complex system of American governance. It's a document that has shaped the lives of millions and influenced countless nations. But, before we dive into the heady debates and landmark amendments, let's start with the basics: the structure of the Constitution itself. It kicks off with the Preamble, an opening statement that lays out the vision and purpose behind this historic document. Then, we get into the nitty-gritty with the first three Articles, establishing the three branches of government: Legislative (Article I), Executive (Article II), and Judicial (Article III). Each has its own unique powers and responsibilities, designed to balance out the others and prevent any single part from becoming too powerful. Next, Articles IV through VII cover the roles of the states, the process for making amendments, and the procedures for ratification. Understanding this structure gives us a solid foundation to explore how these articles and amendments work in real life, affecting everything from the laws we follow to the rights we hold dear. So, let's take this one step at a time, and by the end, you'll see just how this old document is still very much alive and kicking in our modern world.

The Preamble: What It Promises

So, you've just flipped the page from learning about the intriguing backstory of the U.S. Constitution. Now, let's ease into what it sets out at the very beginning - the Preamble. Think of the Preamble as the opening act, setting the stage for everything that follows. It's like the appetizer before the main course, giving us a taste of the Constitution's goals and purposes. Essentially, the Preamble promises a government that aims to ensure justice, peace, protection, and liberty not just for the folks back then but for all generations to come.

Now, "We the People" - these three words are probably among the most famous in American history. They signify that the power and authority of the government don't come from some far-off monarch or select elite. They come directly from us, the people. It's a powerful reminder that in this country, the citizens are the ones calling the shots. This foundational principle is about creating a government that works for its people, striving to serve and protect their interests.

Moving forward, the Preamble talks about establishing "justice" and ensuring "domestic Tranquility." In layman's terms, it's about making sure that fairness is a non-negotiable and that our neighborhoods and communities remain peaceful. It acknowledges that for a society to thrive, there has to be a solid system in place that keeps things fair and peaceful. And let's be honest, who doesn't want to live in a place where justice and peace are top priorities?

Additionally, it touches on providing for the common defense and promoting the general Welfare. This means the government has the responsibility to protect its citizens from outside threats and to create conditions where everyone can prosper. It's not just about having a strong military; it's also about making sure the economy is healthy, people have access to necessary services, and the overall quality of life is constantly improving.

Lastly, the Preamble ensures the "Blessings of Liberty." It's a promise to safeguard our freedom and make sure future generations can enjoy it too. This part is a big deal because it lays the groundwork for a society that values and protects individual freedoms and rights above all. In summary, the Preamble isn't just a fancy introduction; it's a cornerstone, encapsulating the vision of a nation committed to justice, peace, security, and freedom for all its citizens. It sets a high bar, sure, but it's also a constant reminder of what we're striving towards together.

Article I: The Legislative Branch

So, you've made it past the preamble and you're diving into the heart of the Constitution. First stop? Article I, which is all about the Legislative Branch of the U.S. government. This is where laws start their journey, shaped and molded by a group of folks elected to represent the interests of the people. Think of it as the country's law-making factory, consisting of two main parts: the Senate and the House of Representatives.

The House of Representatives is kind of like your local high school's student council but on steroids. Representatives are elected based on the population of each state, meaning more people equals more representatives. These reps serve two-year terms, and they've got the nifty job of initiating bills that can raise revenue. That's right - when it comes to money matters, the House holds the purse strings.

Then there's the Senate, the wise old council where each state, regardless of its size, gets two senators. These folks serve longer terms, six years, allowing them to really sink their teeth into complex issues and long-term policymaking. The Senate has exclusive jobs too, like confirming presidential appointments and ratifying treaties. Together, these two bodies form the Congress, a powerhouse of legislative authority.

Article I doesn't stop at setting up the chessboard; it dives into the rules of the game. It outlines the process by which a bill becomes law, a procedure that requires agreement from both the House and the Senate, followed by the president's signature. Sure, it sounds straightforward, but in practice, it's as challenging as getting a cat to walk on a leash.

This article also spells out the powers granted to Congress, and they're not minor. We're talking about the authority to tax, to declare war, to regulate commerce among the states, and much, much more. Yet, with great power comes great responsibility, and Article I makes it clear that this power cannot be used willy-nilly; certain limits and prohibitions keep the Legislative Branch in check.

But Article I isn't just about handing out power; it's also about drawing lines in the sand. It sets boundaries on what Congress can't do. For instance, passing laws that retroactively punish actions or denying citizens their right to a fair trial are big no-nos. These safeguards ensure that the law-making process respects the rights and liberties of the American people.

In wrapping up, think of Article I as the foundation of a democracy that seeks to represent its citizens' diverse voices through elected individuals. It's a pivotal piece of the constitutional puzzle, designed to ensure that the law of the land is created by the people, for the people. And while it might sound a bit dry, remember, these are the rules of the game that help protect your freedoms and shape your everyday life. So understanding Article I? It's definitely worth your time.

Article II: The Executive Branch

So, we've walked through the halls of Congress in Article I, understanding how laws get made. Next up, let's dive into the world where those laws are enforced, and basically, where the action happens:

the Executive Branch. This branch is all about the President, Vice President, and the Cabinet. Think of it as the management team of the United States.

The big boss, the President, is the face of the executive branch. This role comes with a hefty to-do list, from being the Commander-in-Chief of the armed forces to negotiating treaties with other countries. But it's not a solo act; the President's decisions are often shaped by advice from the Vice President and the Cabinet—think of them as the President's specialized advisory board, each member overseeing different sectors like education, defense, and health.

Now, how does someone even become President? It's not just about having a desire to sit in the Oval Office. The Constitution lays out some clear rules: you've got to be a natural-born citizen, at least 35 years old, and have lived in the U.S. for at least 14 years. And let's not forget about the election process, which is a whole adventure on its own, involving everything from primaries to the Electoral College.

While the President gets a lot of the spotlight, the role of the Vice President shouldn't be overlooked. Originally, the VP's job was to be the understudy, ready to step into the lead role if needed. But over the years, VPs have taken on more responsibilities, often serving as key advisors and taking on special projects.

Running the country isn't a one-person show, and that's where the Cabinet comes in. These folks are the heads of the executive departments and play a crucial role in making sure everything from your local post office to national security is handled. They're the President's go-to experts, bringing insights from their fields to help shape policies and decisions.

But it's not all about making decisions and running the show. The executive branch also has the power of the veto. Picture this: Congress passes a law, but the President says, "I don't think so," and vetoes it.

Congress can still override this veto, but it's a tough climb, needing a two-thirds majority in both houses.

In conclusion, the Executive Branch is where plans set by Congress get put into motion. It's a mix of leadership, decision-making, and action. From the President to the Cabinet, each member plays a critical role in managing the country's affairs, enforcing laws, and guiding the nation through both calm and stormy seas.

Article III: The Judicial Branch

When we talk about the Judicial Branch, we're diving into the world of courts and the interpretation of the law. At the heart of this branch is the Supreme Court, but it's also about a bunch of other courts that deal with federal issues. Basically, this branch makes sure the law is applied correctly and resolves disputes fairly, stepping in when things get murky.

Article III of the U.S. Constitution sets up the Judicial Branch and leaves a lot of room for Congress to fill in the details. It's a bit like saying, "Here's the outline; you fill in the colors." This setup has allowed the judicial system to grow and evolve over time. What started as a simple structure now includes numerous federal courts and specialized courts, like bankruptcy and tax courts, all playing their part in interpreting the law.

The Supreme Court is the big boss in the judiciary world. It's the final stop for legal battles that have made their way through the system, often dealing with the most complex issues. What's cool (and a bit daunting) about the Supreme Court is that its decisions set precedents, meaning they influence or determine the outcomes of future cases. It's like setting the rules of the game that everyone else needs to play by.

One key aspect of Article III is the idea of judicial independence. The framers of the Constitution were pretty smart about this, wanting to make sure judges weren't swayed by changing political winds. That's why federal judges, including Supreme Court justices, keep their jobs "during good Behaviour," which usually means for life, unless they resign, retire, or are removed after being impeached and convicted for serious misconduct. This lifelong appointment helps judges make decisions based on the law, not on what's popular at the moment.

But Article III isn't just about protecting the people in black robes. It also shields the process and principles of fair justice, ensuring that the courts remain a place where law and facts matter more than pressure and influence. This is where concepts like the right to a fair trial and the jurisdiction of federal courts come into play, outlining what kinds of cases they can hear and how they should be conducted.

What's particularly interesting about the Judicial Branch is its role in the balance of powers. It has the power to check the actions of the other two branches through judicial review, which means it can declare laws or executive actions unconstitutional. This might sound like giving a lot of power to the courts, but it's actually a critical part of ensuring no part of the government becomes too powerful. Think of it as the system's built-in balance scale.

So there you have it: the Judicial Branch in a nutshell. It's not just about wearing robes and wielding gavels; it's a fundamental part of how our country's laws are interpreted and applied. By providing a system to resolve disputes and check the powers of the other branches, the Judicial Branch helps maintain the rule of law and protect the rights promised in the Constitution.

Articles IV-VII: The States, Amendments, and Ratification

Transitioning from the branches of government, we dive into the nuts and bolts holding the states together, how the Constitution can change over time, and how all this came to be official. It's like examining the rules of a complex board game, where each state plays its part, new rules can be added, and everything started with an agreement.

Article IV deals with the states in this grand union of ours. Think of it as the Constitution's way of ensuring that states play nice with each other. It talks about respecting each other's laws and court decisions, a bit like ensuring no state acts like it's in its own little world. It also has rules for adding new states to the club because, back in the day, they were eyeing expansion westward. And there's a clause about protecting states against invasions or violence, which sounds pretty dramatic but essential.

Moving onto Article V, this is where the Constitution shows its flexibility. It outlines how amendments, or changes, can be made. This process isn't exactly easy—intentionally so—to prevent constant revisions. You need a lot of agreement (two-thirds of both Congress houses or a special convention) just to propose an amendment. Then, three-fourths of the states must ratify (approve) it. This is how we've gotten additions like the Bill of Rights and other critical amendments over the centuries.

Article VI can be seen as a "this is the ultimate law of the land" statement. It says that the Constitution, and federal laws made under it, trump any state laws. Plus, it requires all officers and judges in the U.S. to swear an oath to support the Constitution, but no religious tests can be required for holding any government position. This solidified the separation of church and state right from the nation's early days.

Finally, Article VII explained how the Constitution itself would be kick-started. It required nine out of the original thirteen states to agree for it to go into effect. Imagine convincing most of a group to agree on where to have dinner; now imagine it's about founding a country's legal system. High stakes, right?

These sections of the Constitution are crucial for understanding the balance of power not just between the branches of government but between the federal government and the states. It's why we can have uniform rules for some things (like trade between states) and different local laws for others (like education or policing).

Amendments have been key to evolving our nation's laws to better reflect current values and knowledge. Without the ability to amend the Constitution, we'd be stuck with rules that might not fit today's society. It's a way of keeping the document alive, relevant, and capable of protecting the rights of its citizens in changing times.

The requirement for ratification, especially the part about needing a supermajority of states, emphasizes the importance of a wide consensus. It's a safeguard against fleeting passions pushing through significant changes, ensuring that amendments have broad support across the country.

Looking at how all this started with the ratification of the Constitution itself reminds us that what we have today was agreed upon by a collective decision. It wasn't dictated or imposed. This collaborative spirit is something that's supposed to continue guiding how the states interact, how the Constitution changes, and how governance is approached.

Understanding Articles IV through VII gives us insight into the Constitution's resilience and adaptability. It's designed to serve a diverse and evolving union, ensuring unity while allowing for change. As we transition into looking more closely at the Amendments themselves in the next chapters, we'll see how this process of change has played out over the centuries, reflecting the nation's growth and the challenges it's faced.

Chapter 2:
The Bill of Rights: A Closer Look

Diving into the Bill of Rights, we're taking a deep breath and going under the surface of what might seem like legal jargon to reveal the gold hidden beneath. This isn't just a list of do's and don'ts. It's the backbone of American freedom, the promises that keep your rights safe from getting nibbled away by the ever-hungry fish of government overreach. We kick off with the First Amendment, which is your ticket to say what you think, pray how you wish, or even critique the government without fear of a knock on your door in the middle of the night. Then there's the Second Amendment, sparking debates hotter than a Fourth of July barbecue about who gets to bear arms and why. Fast forward to amendments like the Fourth, giving you a say on who's allowed to comb through your personal belongings and the Fifth ensuring you can't be bullied into incriminating yourself. These aren't just historical footnotes; they are your shields. The Sixth and Seventh keep fairness front and center in courtrooms, while the Eighth ensures punishments aren't straight out of a horror movie. Ever feel like the Constitution forgot something? That's where the Ninth and Tenth come in, reminding us that the people and states have powers too, powers that aren't scribbled down in this historic document. So, as we lace up our sneakers to walk through each of these rights, remember, they're not just words on a parchment—they're the guardians of your freedom.

Amendment I: Freedoms, Petitions, Assembly

1 Congress shall make no law respecting an establishment of religion, or prohibiting the free exercise thereof; or abridging the freedom of speech, or of the press; or the right of the people peaceably to assemble, and to petition the Government for a redress of grievances.

First up, let's dive into the First Amendment, the starting line of the Bill of Rights and an absolute powerhouse when it comes to protecting our freedoms. It's a bit like a Swiss Army knife for U.S. citizens—packed with essential tools in one compact package. At its core, this amendment protects five fundamental freedoms: speech, religion, press, assembly, and the right to petition the government.

Why lump all these together? Well, they're all about ensuring we can think, believe, and express ourselves without fear of government interference. It's about having conversations, even uncomfortable ones, because that's how societies move forward. It tells us that whether you're whispering in the back of a library or shouting from the rooftops, your voice matters.

Freedom of speech is one you've likely heard a lot about. It means you can voice your opinions, even if they're not popular, without the government stopping you. This freedom isn't absolute (you can't yell "fire" in a crowded theater when there's no fire), but it's pretty broad.

Then there's freedom of religion. This part says you can follow the faith of your choice or none at all. It's a statement that we're not a one-size-fits-all nation when it comes to spirituality. The government won't play favorites with religions, either.

The freedom of the press ensures journalists can dig into stories and share their findings without governmental pressure to keep things under wraps. It's a critical check on power because a well-informed public is necessary for democracy to function properly.

Freedom of assembly? This one's about hanging out. Well, sort of. It means people can come together, publicly or privately, for social, political, or economic reasons. Want to protest a new law or celebrate your heritage? This freedom guarantees you can.

And the right to petition the government is your direct line to those in charge. It's saying, "Hey, we've got something to say about how things are run around here." It's a formal way to express concerns, seek changes, or get answers from government officials.

Now, it's worth mentioning that these freedoms aren't without their gray areas or controversies. Free speech, for instance, is a hot topic, especially on college campuses and social media platforms where the line between hate speech and free speech is hotly debated.

Religious freedom too sparks debates, especially when personal beliefs bump up against laws or policies aimed at ensuring equal treatment for everyone. It's a balancing act between respecting individual beliefs and protecting the rights of all citizens.

Freedom of the press has been under scrutiny as well, with discussions around what constitutes responsible journalism and the rise of "fake news." It's a reminder of the role of the press in a healthy democracy and the need for critical thinking.

As for assembly and petitioning, they remind us that democracy is not a spectator sport. Whether it's a local town hall meeting or a national march, these rights enable people to come together for a common cause and make their voices heard.

So, why do these freedoms matter so much? They're the foundation of a democratic society. Without them, it's hard to imagine the United States as we know it. They ensure a marketplace of ideas, where beliefs and opinions can be shared, tested, and challenged.

It's also about accountability. These rights give citizens the power to question their leaders, to highlight injustices, and to demand better.

They're a check on the power of the government, ensuring it serves the people, not the other way around.

The First Amendment lays the groundwork for innovation and progress. By protecting dissenting voices and new ideas, we've seen social movements flourish, policies change, and society evolve. It's the engine of change that keeps the nation moving forward.

Remember, these rights are not just theoretical. They impact our daily lives, from the news we read, the beliefs we hold, to the protests we see on our streets. They're about having the freedom to explore, to wonder, and to speak out.

Finally, the First Amendment is a reminder of the responsibility each of us holds. With these freedoms comes the duty to exercise them respectfully and to protect them for everyone, even those with whom we strongly disagree. After all, these rights are only as strong as our commitment to uphold them for all.

In conclusion, Amendment I is a powerhouse, defending our most cherished freedoms. It's a constant reminder that in a land brimming with diverse thoughts and beliefs, our strength comes from our ability to express them, to debate them, and ultimately, to coexist with them. It underscores a fundamental truth: that freedom, in all its forms, is essential to the American way of life.

Explained: Your Right to Speak and Worship Freely Zooming in on the First Amendment, it fundamentally secures two critical aspects of democratic life: *the freedom to speak one's mind and the freedom to practice or not practice any religion. At its core, this amendment protects against the government silencing its citizens or dictating their spiritual beliefs.* Let's break this down into something a bit more digestible.

First off, freedom of speech. What does this really mean? In essence, you can express your opinions, whether in writing, art, or a good old-fashioned verbal rant, without fear of government retaliation. It's why protests, debates, and even the criticisms of those in power are a staple of American life. *However, this freedom isn't absolute. There are limits, especially when speech can harm others or threatens national security.* Yet, the default setting is always to encourage open dialogue.

Then there's the freedom of religion aspect. This part of the First Amendment ensures you can follow the religion of your choice or none at all. The government can't coerce you into practicing a specific religion, nor can it punish you for your religious beliefs or lack thereof. This principle establishes what's known as the "separation of church and state," ensuring a secular government that neither favors nor discriminates against any religion.

Why are these freedoms lumped together in the First Amendment? It signals just how fundamental they are to the essence of American democracy. Being able to speak freely encourages a marketplace of ideas, where beliefs and opinions can be openly exchanged and debated. *And ensuring the freedom to follow any religion or none at all protects the conscience of every individual, allowing them to live authentically according to their beliefs.*

It's important to note that while the First Amendment protects these rights on a federal level, there have been cases and controversies over the years about what exactly constitutes protected speech or the extent of religious freedom. For instance, hate speech, while abhorrent, is largely protected under the First Amendment unless it incites immediate violence. Similarly, while you're free to practice your religion, this doesn't allow for practices that harm others or break general laws that apply to everyone.

So, what does this mean for you? Simply put, you can advocate for causes you believe in, express your thoughts on government policies, and practice your religion, all without fear of government intervention. But, remembering that these freedoms work within a framework designed to protect all individuals in society is crucial. It's a balance of liberty and responsibility.

In wrapping up, the First Amendment's assurances of speech and religious freedoms are cornerstones of American democracy. They ensure a society in which individuals can speak their minds and follow their spiritual paths freely, contributing to the vibrant, diverse, and dynamic culture that defines the United States. As citizens and residents, understanding and exercising these rights is not just a privilege but a vital part of participating in and shaping the nation's future.

Amendment II: Right to Bear Arms

2 A well regulated Militia, being necessary to the security of a free state, the right of the people to keep and bear Arms, shall not be infringed.

Jumping straight into the Second Amendment, you might hear a lot about it regarding debates on gun control and individual rights. At its core, this amendment grants Americans the right to own guns. Back in the day when this was written, folks felt strongly about having the means to protect themselves and their property, not just from burglars or wild animals, but also from the possibility of a tyrannical government. What this means for you today is that you're allowed to own a firearm, but with certain regulations and rules depending on where you live. It's like having a driver's license: you've got the right to drive, but you need to follow the traffic laws. Similarly, owning a gun comes with its own set of responsibilities and laws aimed at keeping everyone safe. This discussion about how we balance individual rights with public safety is ongoing, keeping the Second Amendment at the forefront of political and legal debates.

Explained: What This Means for You Now, talking about the Second Amendment, it's about more than just the words on a page. It's about understanding how those words translate to everyday life for people from all walks of life. At its core, the Second Amendment gives individuals the right to bear arms. But what does that look like in 2023? It means different things depending on who you ask, and where you're asking it.

For starters, this right ensures that you have the ability to own a firearm for personal use. That includes protection, hunting, and sports shooting. The interpretation of this can vary widely across states, which have their own laws that can either broaden or narrow down this right. So, while the constitution gives you this right, your local laws are going to play a big part in determining what that actually looks like day to day.

This amendment's relevance in today's society often sparks a deep and sometimes divisive conversation about gun control, public safety, and personal freedoms. It's a debate that touches on the role of government, the need for safety measures, and where the line between public safety and individual rights should be drawn. This is something to be aware of because the debates and laws that come from these conversations can directly impact you - whether it's in the form of background checks, waiting periods, or restrictions on certain types of firearms.

Understanding the Second Amendment also means recognizing its historical context and how that shapes today's interpretations. Originally part of ensuring a militia's capability, today, it supports the notion of individual rights to gun ownership. This evolution in interpretation shows how the Constitution is a living document, one that adapts and changes with the times, reflecting current values and societal needs.

To you, this might mean reassurance in your right to protect your home, or it could mean frustration if you feel that gun laws are not strict enough. It's essential to keep informed about your state's laws and the national conversation around gun rights and regulation. Your voice and vote can influence how this amendment is applied and interpreted, ensuring it aligns with contemporary standards of safety and freedom.

For those not interested in owning firearms, this amendment still impacts you through the national and local policies on public safety and crime. It's a significant part of the broader discussion on how to balance rights with responsibilities, a conversation that affects communities and law enforcement practices.

Lastly, remember that engaging in this conversation, regardless of where you stand, is part of your civic duty. Understanding the Second Amendment—and all parts of the Constitution—allows for a more informed citizenry capable of contributing to meaningful discussions on our rights, freedoms, and responsibilities. It's not just about knowing your rights but understanding the implications they have on the fabric of our society.

Amendment III: Quartering of Soldiers

3 No soldier shall, in time of peace be quartered in any house, without the consent of the owner, nor in time of war, but in a manner to be prescribed by law.

Imagine coming home to find soldiers chilling on your couch, eating your food, and telling you it's their right to stay there because the government said so. Well, back in the day, this wasn't just a wild thought; it was reality until the Third Amendment stepped in and said, "Nope, not happening." In simple terms, this part of the Bill of Rights makes sure that the government can't force you to let soldiers live in your house without your okay, except in super rare cases, and even then, they'd have to do it in a way that's fair and follows the law. It's one of those amendments we don't talk about much today because, let's be honest, it did its job so well back then that we don't really worry about soldiers crashing at our places uninvited anymore. But it's a cool reminder of how the folks who put together the Bill of Rights were thinking about all the ways to keep people's homes safe from government intrusion.

Explained: No Soldiers in Your Home Without Consent So, you've probably never thought you'd wake up to find soldiers making themselves at home in your living room. But back in the day, this was a real worry. Imagine, after a long day, you come back to your place, and there's an entire squad chilling on your couch, eating your food, and there's not much you can do about it. That's why the Third Amendment of the U.S. Constitution was a big deal when it was penned. It basically says, "Nope, can't happen" unless you, the homeowner, give the OK.

This amendment might seem a bit outdated or unnecessary today, but context is everything. The folks who drafted the Constitution had a clear memory of British soldiers taking over homes whenever they felt like it during the Colonial era. It was their way of saying that personal privacy and property rights are fundamental. It assures us that our homes are our sanctuaries, free from being unwillingly turned into military barracks. The idea is simple yet powerful: your home is your castle, and the government can't just invade that space.

The beauty of the Third Amendment, though, isn't just about the protection it offers against a very specific kind of government intrusion. It sets a precedent for the broader concept of privacy and personal freedom. It's part of the Bill of Rights, a cornerstone in establishing boundaries for government reach against individual liberties. Even if the thought of soldiers in your living room is far-fetched today, the amendment reinforces the principle that there are limits to government power. It underscores the importance of consent and autonomy in spaces we consider private and personal. Even in a modern context where the "soldiers" might be metaphorical, this amendment reminds us that our rights to personal space and privacy are worth protecting.

Amendment IV: Searches and Seizures

4 The right of the people to be secure in their persons, houses, papers, and effects, against unreasonable searches and seizures, shall not be violated, and no Warrants shall issue, but upon probable cause, supported by Oath or Affirmation, and particularly describing the place to be searched, and the persons or things to be seized.

When it comes to Amendment IV, we're looking at your right to a little privacy. Think about it like this: You've got your own space, your house, your car, your backpack, and it's yours, right? You wouldn't want someone rummaging through it without a good reason. Well, the Fourth Amendment is your constitutional shield; it says that you have the right to be secure in your personal spaces. This means the police can't just decide to search your things or take your stuff without a warrant—a special permission slip from a judge, saying they have a solid reason to believe you've got some evidence of a crime in there. And getting this warrant isn't just a formality; the judge needs proof, something more substantial than a hunch or a rumor. So, if you ever feel like someone's stepping over the line into your privacy without a good reason or proper authorization, remember, the Fourth Amendment's got your back, ensuring your personal space is respected and protected.

Explained: Your Privacy and the Police Getting into the nitty-gritty of the Fourth Amendment, it's like having a personal shield against undue hassle by the boys and girls in blue. Here's the deal: the Fourth Amendment guards you against unwarranted searches and seizures. This means the police can't just barge into your life - be it your house, car, or personal effects - without a good reason, typically needing a warrant from a judge, which itself requires probable cause.

So, what's 'probable cause'? In plain speak, it's a reasonable basis to believe a crime has been, is being, or is about to be committed. It's not just a hunch or a guess. Police need concrete evidence or a strong suspicion based on facts. This concept is a cornerstone of your privacy rights. Without it, any police officer could search anyone at any time, for any reason, or no reason at all.

However, like most rules, there are exceptions. For instance, if a police officer has a valid reason to believe someone's in immediate danger, or if evidence is about to be destroyed, they might not need a warrant. It's a fine line between safeguarding public safety and protecting individual rights. That's why disputes about searches and seizures often end up in court.

Technology today presents new challenges. Back when the Constitution was written, "papers and effects" meant just that. But now, it includes your digital life too - emails, texts, and social media activity can all be considered under the umbrella of privacy protected by the Fourth Amendment. The courts are still working out how modern tech fits into ancient protections.

What does this all mean for you? In simple terms, if the police want to search your property or seize your stuff, they generally need to convince a judge there's a good reason for it. And if you feel your privacy's been invaded unlawfully you have the right to challenge that in court. Your privacy rights ensure there's a legal process that must be followed, one that's designed to protect you against arbitrary or unjustifiable intrusions by the state.

Remember, though, rights come with responsibilities. Knowing the basics of what the police can and cannot do can help you navigate interactions with them more confidently. But also bear in mind, if you give consent for a search, the need for a warrant goes out the window. So, understanding your rights is key to maintaining your privacy and ensuring your interactions with the police are conducted fairly and lawfully.

Lastly, while the Fourth Amendment offers robust protections, it's not a catch-all shield. It assures a balance between individual privacy and the need for law enforcement to keep us safe. It's a living part of the Constitution, continually interpreted by the courts to address the evolving nature of privacy and policing, especially in our digital age. So, staying informed about your rights is more important than ever.

Amendment V: Rights in Criminal Cases

5 No person shall be held to answer for a capital , or otherwise infamous crime, unless on a presentment or indictment of a Grand Jury, except in cases arising in the land or naval forces, or in the Militia, when in actual service in time of war or public danger; nor shall any person by subject for the same offence to be twice put in jeopardy in life or limb; nor shall nor be compelled in any criminal case to be a witness to himself, nor be deprived of life, liberty, or property, without the process of law; nor shall private property be taken for public use, without just compensation.

Getting wrapped up in legal troubles isn't something anyone plans for. When it happens, though, the Fifth Amendment is like the safety net that catches you. Imagine you're accused of a crime; this part of the Bill of Rights makes sure you're not pressured to testify against yourself—ever heard the phrase "pleading the Fifth"? That's where it comes from. It also guarantees a few other fair-play rules: You won't face trial for a serious offense without a grand jury deciding there's enough evidence, and you can't be tried twice for the same crime if you were already cleared (that's called "double jeopardy"). Plus, the government can't just take your stuff, whether it's your house or your backyard, without a good reason and without paying you what it's worth. And importantly, it insists on due process, meaning the law has to treat you fairly through every step of the process. So, the Fifth Amendment is basically your shield, making sure you're treated justly, your words can't be twisted against you, and that your property is your own unless there's a very good reason—and compensation.

Explained: Protection Against Self-Incrimination and More
Let's dive into one of the shiny pearls of the Fifth Amendment: protection against self-incrimination. Ever heard someone say, "I plead the Fifth"? That's it – the golden ticket to not having to answer questions that might make you look guilty of a crime. But why's that so important, and what else does the Fifth Amendment cover? Pull up a chair; let's break it down.

The Fifth Amendment is like a Swiss Army knife for people in the hot seat legally. Besides protection against self-incrimination, it also promises due process of law, shields against double jeopardy (being tried for the same crime twice), and ensures fair compensation when the government takes your property for public use. Sounds like a lot, right? It's basically saying, "We've got your back" when it comes to the potential overreach of legal authorities.

Let's talk about the no-self-snitch rule, officially known as protection against self-incrimination. Imagine you're in court, and there's a situation where answering honestly could make you look guilty. Instead of having to choose between lying (which is a no-no) and incriminating yourself, the Fifth Amendment allows you to opt-out, keeping silent as your right. This keeps the justice system fair, making it the government's job to prove you're guilty, not your job to prove you're innocent.

Then there's due process of law, another gem in the Fifth. This means the government can't just decide to take away your life, freedom, or property without following the law to the letter. It's like a reminder to the powers that be: "Hey, don't forget to cross your T's and dot your I's before you try to penalize someone."

Double jeopardy might sound like a game show, but in the Fifth Amendment, it's serious business. Once you're tried for a crime and found not guilty, you can't be dragged back into court for the same offense. It's the law's way of saying, "Case closed, no do-overs." This ensures that trials are conducted fairly and that verdicts are final, protecting individuals from endless legal battles over the same charge.

Ever wonder about the government taking private property for stuff like roads or parks? That's where the term "eminent domain" comes into play, and yes, the Fifth Amendment covers that too. It says that if the government needs your property for public use, they can take it, but not without giving you proper compensation. It's a balance between public needs and individual rights.

The Fifth Amendment serves as a cornerstone of legal protections in the United States. Whether it's shielding against self-incrimination, enforcing due process, preventing double jeopardy, or ensuring fair compensation for eminent domain, the Fifth's got you covered. It exemplifies the Constitution's commitment to balancing government power with individual freedoms, making sure that in the pursuit of justice, fairness is never compromised.

Amendment VI: Right to a Fair Trial

6 In all criminal prosecutions, the accused shall enjoy the right to a speedy and public trial, by an impartial jury of the state and district wherein the crime shall have been committed, which district shall have been previously ascertained by law, and to be informed of the nature and cause of the accusation; to be confronted with the witnesses against him; to have compulsory process for obtaining witnesses in his favor, and to have the Assistance of Counsel for his defence.

Imagine you're accused of stealing a cookie from the cookie jar, but you know you didn't do it. You'd want a chance to clear your name, right? That's what Amendment VI in the U.S. Bill of Rights is all about - ensuring you get a fair trial if you're ever in hot water legally. It guarantees a bunch of important rights to make sure the trial is fair: you have the right to know why you're being accused, the right to have a lawyer to help argue your side (even if you can't afford one, the court appoints one for you), the right to see and hear the evidence against you, and the chance to tell your side of the story. It also says your trial has to happen quickly, in a place where the crime was committed, and in front of an impartial jury - that means the jury can't start off thinking you're guilty or have it out for you. This amendment is a big deal because it tries to make sure that everyone, no matter who they are, gets a fair shake in court. It's about protecting the little guy and making sure the justice system is just, which is pretty core to what America stands for.

Explained: Your Rights in the Courtroom Let's dive into a topic that might seem daunting at first but is crucial for everyone to understand: your rights in the courtroom. Imagine you find yourself in a situation where you need to defend yourself in court. Knowing your rights can be the shield and sword that protect you and ensure you're treated fairly.

The Sixth Amendment of the U.S. Constitution packs a lot into a few lines. It guarantees some critical rights for anyone accused of a crime. First off, you have the right to a speedy and public trial. This means the government can't keep you waiting years for a trial, and they can't do it in secret, either. The idea is to prevent injustice through unnecessary delays or hidden courtroom shenanigans.

Then, there's the right to an impartial jury. This is your safeguard against biased decisions – the jury is supposed to be made up of people from your community, without any preconceptions about your guilt or innocence. But it's not just about having a jury; the Sixth Amendment also gives you the right to know who's accusing you, the nature of the charges and evidence against you, and it compels witnesses to show up and speak in your defense if necessary.

Perhaps one of the most crucial rights is the right to an attorney. If you can't afford one, the state must provide one for you. This ensures that everyone has the opportunity to be defended properly, not just those who can pay for the best defense money can buy. It's a cornerstone of ensuring fairness in our judicial system, aiming to level the playing field.

But what does all this really mean for you? In simple terms, if you're ever in a sticky situation where you're facing charges, these rights are like your personal set of tools to help you navigate the waters of the legal system. They're designed to protect you from unfair treatment and ensure you get a fair shot at defending yourself.

Understanding these rights is not just about knowing what happens in courtroom dramas on TV; it's about recognizing the protections the Constitution guarantees you if you ever need them. It means having the knowledge to demand fair treatment and the confidence to question anything that seems unjust.

In conclusion, the Sixth Amendment and your rights in the courtroom embody principles of fairness, equality, and justice. By grasping these concepts, you're better prepared to stand up for yourself and others, ensuring that the scales of justice are balanced for all. So, while we all hope never to have to defend ourselves in court, understanding these rights is a powerful part of being an informed citizen.

Amendment VII: Rights in Civil Cases

7 In suits of common law, where the value in controversy shall exceed twenty dollars, the right of trial be jury shall be preserved, and no fact

tried by a jury shall be otherwise re-examined in any court in the United States, than according to the rules of the common law.

Jumping into the Seventh Amendment, we're talking about your right to have a trial by jury in certain civil cases. This might sound a bit formal, but really, it's about keeping things fair when there's a dispute over money or property that's worth more than 20 dollars. Back when this was written, 20 bucks was a lot more than it is today, but the principle still stands. Instead of letting a single judge have all the say, this amendment makes sure a group of regular folks can weigh in, bringing community judgment into the courtroom. It's like having a bunch of friends help decide who's right in an argument, except these friends are randomly selected and don't know either person. This ensures the decision is impartial and reflects common sense. Plus, once the jury makes a decision, it's pretty hard for anyone to overturn it without a good reason. So, we're talking about a powerful way to keep things square and fair when people disagree over stuff that matters to them.

Explained: Trials by Jury in Civil Cases Let's dive into the Seventh Amendment, which emphasizes the right to a jury trial in civil cases. Now, civil cases are different from criminal ones since they usually involve disputes between people or organizations regarding the legal duties and responsibilities they owe one another. Think of someone suing another over a contract dispute or a property boundary issue.

The Seventh Amendment is like the quieter cousin of the Sixth Amendment, which guarantees the right to a jury in criminal trials. Why does this matter, you might ask? Well, it's about ensuring that even in disputes that don't involve a crime, you've got the fairness of a group of your peers deciding on the matter. This keeps a single judge from holding all the power over the case's outcome, promoting a balanced and democratic process.

Here's the catch, though. The amendment specifies that the case must involve a claim exceeding twenty dollars for the jury trial right to kick in. While twenty dollars doesn't sound like much today, back when this part of the Constitution was written, twenty bucks was a significant sum. It's a way of saying that the issue has to be substantial enough to warrant a jury's involvement.

One fascinating aspect of the Seventh Amendment is how it connects the present with the past. It demands that common law - essentially, law developed from judicial decisions and customs over time - be the basis in jury cases. This link to history ensures that modern decisions are grounded in long-standing legal principles, providing continuity and stability in the legal system.

But don't think that a jury in a civil case will sort out every minor detail. Their role is primarily to look at the facts of the case. The legal nuances, that's for the judge to interpret. This division of labor, so to speak, ensures that the trial is both fair and efficient. The jurors apply common sense to the facts before them, while the judge makes sure the trial runs according to the established law.

Yet, despite the value of jury trials in civil cases, it's worth noting that most civil disputes are settled out of court. Why? Well, trials can be costly, lengthy, and unpredictable. Both parties might prefer a settlement that offers a sure outcome, rather than rolling the dice with a jury. However, the right to a jury keeps the system honest, ensuring that such settlements are fair, as the possibility of a trial by jury looms in the background as a powerful motivator for resolution.

To wrap it up, the Seventh Amendment's provision for jury trials in civil cases is a critical aspect of the American judicial system. It safeguards the democratic process, promotes fair outcomes, and links present-day justice with our legal history. It's one of those rights that might not make headlines every day, but it's fundamental to ensuring justice and fairness in the civil disputes that can arise in everyday life.

Amendment VIII: Bails, Fines, and Punishments

8 Excessive bail shall not be required, nor excessive fines imposed, nor cruel and unusual punishments inflicted.

Imagine you're in a spot of trouble. You wouldn't want the punishment to be way harsher than the crime, right? That's exactly what the Eighth Amendment is about. It's like a big protective umbrella ensuring things don't get out of hand when it comes to bails, fines, and punishments. This amendment keeps things fair, stating that you can't be slapped with excessive bail or fines, and as for punishments, forget about cruel and unusual ones—those are a big no-no. Let's say you were caught spray-painting a wall. You wouldn't expect to pay a million dollars for bail or face a punishment that's way out of line with the crime. This part of the Bill of Rights is super important because it upholds a fundamental principle of justice: punishment should fit the crime, and everyone deserves to be treated with humanity, even when they've made a mistake.

Explained: Preventing Excessive Punishments When we're talking about keeping punishments from getting out of hand, we're diving straight into the Eighth Amendment. This part of the Constitution is like a guardrail, helping to ensure that when someone breaks the law, the punishment fits the crime without going overboard. In simple terms, it's the part that says the government can't make someone pay an insanely high bail or fine, and it can't hand down cruel or unusual punishment. Think of it as the Constitution's way of saying, "Let's keep things fair and humane, folks."

Now, what exactly counts as excessive or cruel and unusual? That's been up for debate over the years, and it often changes with the times. Historically, punishments that were once seen as acceptable can become viewed as barbaric by modern standards. This shows that our understanding of what's "cruel and unusual" evolves as society does.

So, this amendment isn't just about the past; it's also about adapting to the present and future.

The reason this amendment is so crucial is that it touches directly on human dignity. By preventing excessive bail, fines, and punishments, the Eighth Amendment acknowledges that everyone, even those who've made mistakes, deserves to be treated with basic respect. It's a reminder that the justice system's aim isn't just to punish, but also to rehabilitate and ensure that justice is served in a way that's fair and doesn't degrade human dignity.

One might wonder how this applies in day-to-day life. For starters, it means that if someone you know is facing legal trouble, there are constitutional protections in place to prevent their punishment from being disproportionately harsh compared to the crime. It's also a critical standard that legal professionals and judges must adhere to, ensuring that the sentences they hand down are not only lawful but just. This safeguard helps maintain trust in the legal system, ensuring it serves justice rather than vengeance.

In wrapping up, the Eighth Amendment and its stance against excessive punishments highlight a fundamental value: even in the face of wrongdoing, human rights should be upheld. It stands as a testament to the idea that justice should be served with a sense of humanity, keeping punishments from becoming a tool for undue harshness. As we navigate through the complexities of modern society, this principle continues to guide and shape our understanding of justice, ensuring it remains balanced and fair.

Amendment IX: Rights Retained by the People

9 The enumeration in the Constitution, of certain rights, shall not be construed to deny or disparage others retained by the people.

Ever feel like you've got more freedoms than what's written down on paper? Well, you're spot on, and Amendment IX of the U.S.

Constitution makes it clear. In simple terms, this amendment means just because a right isn't mentioned in the Constitution doesn't mean it doesn't exist. Think of it as the Constitution's way of saying, "Hey, we've listed some key rights, but we know we can't think of everything. So, if it's not in here, you still might have that right." It's like a safety net ensuring that government knows it can't step on unmentioned rights just because they didn't make the list. This is crucial because it stops the government from assuming too much power and keeps our freedoms wide-ranging, not boxed in by a checklist. So, when you're pondering your rights, remember the Ninth Amendment as your reminder that there's more to your freedoms than just the written word.

Explained: Your Rights Aren't Limited by the Constitution
When you think about the Constitution, you might imagine it as a box that holds all your rights, nice and neat. But guess what? It's more like a wide-open field than a closed-off box. The Ninth Amendment makes this crystal clear. It says that just because some rights are listed in the Constitution, it doesn't mean those are the only rights you have.

Let's break it down a bit more. You know how sometimes, when you're telling a story, you can't mention every single detail? Well, the Founding Fathers faced a similar issue. They realized they couldn't list every single right because, frankly, it would be impossible. They wanted to make sure that just because a right wasn't written down, it didn't mean it wasn't protected. So, they included the Ninth Amendment to cover all the bases.

This is crucial because it acknowledges our rights go beyond what's on paper. For example, the right to privacy isn't explicitly mentioned in the Constitution, but over time, courts have recognized it as a fundamental right deeply rooted in several amendments.

What's exciting about this is it shows our understanding of rights isn't static. It can evolve. The Ninth Amendment is like a tool that lets the Constitution grow with society, adapting to new understandings of what freedoms are essential to us.

Some folks might worry this could lead to making up rights willy-nilly, but that's not the case. The process of recognizing new rights is careful and considers history, tradition, and precedent. It's not about pulling rights out of thin air; it's about acknowledging the essential dignity and liberty of individuals in ways that might not have been clear before.

This also means you play a part in shaping what rights are recognized. Through advocacy, discussion, and even court cases, the public helps to define the unwritten rights that the Ninth Amendment protects.

It's like having a garden where the Constitution is the fence around it. The Ninth Amendment reminds us that just because the fence is there, it doesn't mean we can't plant flowers outside of it. Our rights are not limited to the structured garden plots but extend into the fields beyond.

Understanding this amendment teaches us the importance of looking beyond the text and appreciating the broader principles of liberty and justice. It encourages us to think about the spirit of the Constitution – the underlying values that guide the interpretation of all its parts.

So, when you hear talk about constitutional rights, remember the vastness of that concept. The Constitution serves not as a limit but as a launchpad, ensuring that as our society evolves, so too can our recognition of rights. This is a testament to the foresight of the framers and the enduring strength of the document they created.

At the end of the day, the Constitution and its amendments, including the Ninth, are about securing the blessings of liberty. They affirm that our rights are broad, vast, and evolving, and that's something truly worth celebrating.

Amendment X: States' Rights

10 The powers not delegated to the United States by the Constitution, nor prohibited by it to the states, are reserved to the states respectively, or to the people.

Let's dive into the Tenth Amendment, which is all about the balance of power in the USA. Imagine the federal government as a big umbrella; it covers a lot but not everything. The Tenth Amendment is like saying, "Hey, if we didn't specifically say the federal government can do something, then that power stays with the states or the people living there." It's a bit like a safety net, ensuring that the federal government doesn't get too bossy, keeping some decisions closer to home where states can tailor policies to better fit their residents. This means things like education, local law enforcement, and zoning laws are primarily up to states since the Constitution doesn't hand those powers to the federal government. It's like the framers of the Constitution were saying, "We trust the states and their people to handle their business unless we've said otherwise." So, in a nutshell, the Tenth Amendment champions the idea that not all decisions should be made at the highest level of government, which really underscores the importance of states in the federalist system of the United States.

Explained: Powers Not Given to the Federal Government

So, we've reached a spot in our exploration of the Constitution where it's time to talk about limits, specifically the limits of federal power. Think of the federal government as a strong, but not all-powerful, entity; its strengths lie within boundaries. The Tenth Amendment is where the Constitution spells out a crucial balance between state and federal powers. Here's the deal: if the Constitution doesn't give a power to the federal government and doesn't deny it to the states, that power is reserved for the states or the people themselves.

Understanding this is like realizing not all decisions are made from the top down. Picture the U.S. as a team, where the federal government is the coach, but the players - the states and the people - have significant roles that the coach can't just override. The founding fathers designed it this way to ensure a balance of power, preventing too much concentration at the federal level.

Now, why does this matter to you? It means that many laws affecting your daily life - from education to law enforcement to land use - are made at the state or local level. This system allows for diversity in law and policy that matches the diversity of the American public. Different states can have different rules, and that's not only okay, it's by design.

Some critics argue that this can lead to confusion or inconsistency, especially when states have laws that starkly contrast with neighbors'. However, supporters counter that this flexibility is America's strength, permitting experimentation and innovation in governance. Remember, the U.S. is vast; what works in New York might not fly in Nebraska.

At its core, the Tenth Amendment highlights the principle of federalism - a type of government where power is divided between a central authority and constituent political units. It's about balance and respecting the notion that not all solutions come from the top. This balance ensures that local voices and preferences are heard, not drowned out by a one-size-fits-all federal approach.

Let's dive into an example to make this clearer. Consider marijuana laws. Since the federal government hasn't explicitly legalized or criminalized it across the board, states have the flexibility to experiment with their approaches to regulation. Some have legalized it for medical use, others for recreational use, and some have kept it illegal. This patchwork approach showcases the Tenth Amendment in action, allowing states to serve as "laboratories of democracy."

Now, it's essential to note that this balance of power is constantly evolving. The federal government can influence states through federal funding incentives or mandates. For example, the drinking age is set by each state, yet the federal government influenced a nationwide minimum drinking age of 21 by tying federal highway funds to this benchmark.

In sum, while the federal government has considerable power, it's not unlimited. The Tenth Amendment serves as a reminder and protector of states' rights and individual freedoms. It underscores the idea that the U.S. Constitution is not just about granting power, but about limiting it to protect liberty.

So next time you see variation in state laws or policies, remember the Tenth Amendment at work. It's a foundational piece of America's constitutional democracy, ensuring that power is spread out and not hoarded at the top. It's about empowering states and their residents to tailor solutions that best fit their needs, within the country's grander framework.

Chapter 3:
Amendments XI to XXVII:
Extending Liberty and Justice

11 The Judicial power of the United States shall not be construed to extend to any suit in law or equity, commenced or prosecuted against one of the United States by Citizens of another State, or by Citizens or Subjects of any Foreign State.

12 The Electors shall meet in their respective states and vote by ballot for President and Vice President, one of whom, at least, shall not be an inhabitant of the same state with themselves; they shall name in their ballots the person voted for as President, and in distinct ballots the person voted for as Vice-President, and they shall make distinct lists of all persons voted for as President, and of all persons voted for as Vice-President, and of the number of votes for each, which lists they shall sign and certify, and transmit sealed to the seat of the government of the United States, directed to the President of the Senate;--the President of the Senate shall, in the presence of the Senate of House of Representatives, open all the certificates and the votes shall then be counted;--The person having the greatest number of votes for President, if such number be a majority of the whole number of Electors appointed; and if no person have such majority, then from the persons having the highest numbers not exceeding three on the list of those voted for as President, the House of Representatives shall choose immediately, by ballot, the President. But in choosing the President, the votes hall be taken by states, the representation from each state

having one vote; a quorum for this purpose shall consist of a member or members from two-thirds of the states, and a majority of all the states shall be necessary to a choice. (And if the House of Representatives shall not choose a President whenever the right of choice shall devolve upon them before the fourth day of March next following, then the Vice-President shall act as President, as in case of the death or other constitutional disability of the President.--) The person having the greatest number of votes as Vice-President, shall be the Vice-President, if such number be a majority of the whole number of Electors appointed, and if no person have a majority, then from the two highest numbers on the list, the Senate shall choose the Vice-President; a quorum for the purpose shall be necessary to a choice, But no person constitutionally ineligible to the office of President shall be eligible to the of Vice-President of the United States.

So, we've talked about the foundation and the framework—the meat and potatoes of the Constitution, if you will. Now, let's dive into the garden where liberty and justice have grown and flourished over the years through Amendments XI to XXVII. Think of these amendments as the Constitution's way of keeping up with the times, ensuring that the ideals of liberty and justice aren't just fancy words in old documents but living, breathing principles that evolve as we do. From tackling the complexities of lawsuits against states and refining the electoral college in Amendments XI and XII, we've made big leaps toward a more inclusive society. The abolishment of slavery with Amendment XIII and the promise of equal protection under the law in Amendment XIV mark monumental steps toward dismantling centuries of injustice. But the journey didn't stop there; voting rights were expanded regardless of race, gender, and age through Amendments XV, XIX, and XXVI, respectively, underscoring the belief that a democracy thrives only when it listens to all its voices. Interestingly, we've also tinkered with the operational aspects of governance, like income tax (XVI), direct election of senators (XVII), and even how we manage presidential transitions and disabilities (Amendments XX and XXV). Prohibition made its debut and exit in Amendments XVIII and XXI, showing that sometimes, the path to progress involves learning from our missteps. And finally, with the latest, the XXVII Amendment, we've put a check on congressional pay, ensuring those who make the laws don't unfairly benefit from them immediately. Each of these amendments tells a story of struggle, adaptation, and progression, highlighting our nation's ongoing quest to extend liberty and justice for all.

Amendments XI and XII: Lawsuits Against States and Electoral College

So, we've made it to the part of the Constitution that talks about what happens when someone wants to sue a state and how the president gets elected. It might sound dull, but trust me, these amendments have had a big impact on the country.

The Eleventh Amendment came about because of a Supreme Court case, Chisholm v. Georgia, back in 1793. Before this amendment, if you, yes you, had a problem with a state – let's say Georgia owed you money – you could take that state to the Supreme Court. Georgia wasn't too happy being dragged to court like that, and neither were other states. So, the Eleventh Amendment was created to say, "Hold up, you can't sue a state in federal court without its consent." It basically put up a "No Trespassing" sign on each state for certain lawsuits.

Then there's the Twelfth Amendment, which shook up the presidential election process. Originally, the guy with the most votes became president, and the runner-up became vice president. Sounds simple, right? Well, the election of 1800 proved it was anything but. Thomas Jefferson and Aaron Burr tied in the Electoral College, leading to a major headache and a lot of political drama. To avoid future chaos, the Twelfth Amendment said, "Let's have separate ballots for president and vice president." This way, what happened in 1800 wouldn't happen again.

So, what's the big deal with these amendments? Well, the Eleventh Amendment shows us that the relationship between the federal government and the states is complex and requires a balance of power. It's like a dance where sometimes you step forward, and sometimes you step back. It acknowledges that states have their own sovereignty, which is a fancy way of saying they have rights and powers that should be respected.

The Twelfth Amendment, on the other hand, refined the Electoral College system. It didn't get rid of it, but it made sure that the process of choosing a president was clearer and, hopefully, fairer. This amendment underscores the importance of evolving our systems and rules to work better over time. It's a reminder that sometimes, we have to adjust our strategies to make sure everything runs smoothly.

Both of these amendments highlight how the U.S. Constitution is a living document. It's not set in stone. It can be updated and amended to reflect changing times and needs. Think of it like updating software on your phone – it's necessary to keep things working right.

Another interesting point is that these amendments show the balance of power in action. They reflect a thoughtful consideration of how to handle disputes, whether between individuals and states with the Eleventh Amendment or clarifying the roles in the executive branch with the Twelfth. It demonstrates that the Constitution isn't just a set of rules but a framework for navigating the complex realities of governing a diverse and dynamic country.

In essence, the Eleventh and Twelfth Amendments are about making the system work better for everyone. They are about learning from the past – from our mistakes and challenges – and making adjustments to improve. This is what it means to have a living Constitution, one that adapts and grows with us.

While these amendments may not grab headlines like freedom of speech or the right to bear arms, they are critical pieces of the puzzle that is the United States. They help ensure that our government remains functional, respects the sovereignty of states, and evolves with the times. So, next time you hear about the Electoral College or a state being sued, you'll know there's a whole history and a couple of important amendments behind those stories.

In closing, the Eleventh and Twelfth Amendments are like the unsung heroes of the Constitution. They work behind the scenes to keep our country's legal and political systems in check. It's a reminder that every part of the Constitution, no matter how technical or specific, plays a role in shaping the nation and our experience as Americans.

So there you have it, a rundown of two key amendments that help define the balance of power within our federal system and ensure that as times change, our methods of electing leaders and resolving disputes evolve too. It's all part of the grand experiment that is democracy in the United States.

Amendment XIII: Abolition of Slavery

13 **Section 1** Neither slavery nor involuntary servitude except as a punishment for crime whereof the party shall have been duly convicted, shall exist within the United States, or any place subject to their jurisdiction.

Section 2 Congress shall have power to enforce this article by appropriate legislation.

When we talk about the 13th Amendment, we're diving deep into one of the most pivotal moments in American history. This isn't just a line in a legal document; it's the moment the United States officially said no to slavery. Enacted in 1865, this amendment marks a seismic shift in how people are viewed and treated under the law. It declares, in no uncertain terms, that slavery and involuntary servitude are not allowed in the United States, except as punishment for a crime where the person has been duly convicted. This was a big deal because, up until this point, slavery was a deeply entrenched part of American society and economy.

Understanding the 13th Amendment doesn't require a law degree. Imagine living in a time and place where not everyone is free to live their life as they see fit. For centuries, that was the reality for millions of people in the United States. But with the passage of this amendment, the foundation was laid for a new era of freedom and civil rights. It didn't magically solve all the problems overnight—far from it. There were still enormous struggles for equality and justice that followed. But what it did was create a legal baseline that said enslaving another person is not just wrong; it's against the core laws that govern this country.

It's important to note that while the 13th Amendment abolished slavery, it introduced the caveat of punishment for crime, leading to a complex legacy. This clause has been a subject of discussion and critique for how it's been applied throughout history, contributing to debates around the justice system and mass incarceration. However, the core achievement of the amendment—ending legal slavery in the United States—remains a monumental step towards liberty and justice.

In terms of real impact, the 13th Amendment transformed millions of lives. Imagine the profound change for people who, for the first time, could claim their freedom as a right, not a privilege granted by someone else. Families torn apart by slavery now had hope of reuniting and building a future on their terms. It was a moment of immense promise and, at the same time, the beginning of a new and difficult journey towards equality.

So, when we talk about the 13th Amendment, we're acknowledging a turning point that redefined freedom in America. It's not just about the legal prohibition of slavery; it's a testament to the country's ability to evolve and address its deepest flaws. And while the journey towards true equality and justice is ongoing, the 13th Amendment stands as a beacon of hope and a reminder of the power of collective action to effect profound change in society.

Amendment XIV: Citizenship and Equal Protection

14 **Section 1**. All persons born or naturalized in the United States, and subject to the jurisdiction there-of, are citizens of the United States and the State wherein they reside, No States and of the State wherein they reside, No State shall make or enforce any law which shall abridge the privileges or immunities of citizens of the United States, nor shall any State deprive any person of life, liberty, or property, without due process of law; nor deny to any person within its jurisdiction the equal protection of the laws.

Section 2. Representatives shall be apportioned among the several States according to their respective numbers, counting the whole number of persons in each State, excluding Indians not taxed. But when the right to vote at any election for the choice of electors for President and Vice-President of the United States, Representatives in Congress, the Executive and Judicial officers of a State, or the members of the Legislature thereof, is denied to any of the male inhabitants of such State, being twenty-one years of age, and citizens of the United States, or in any way abridged, except for participation in the rebellion, or other crimes, the bases of representation therein shall be reduced in the proportion which the number of such male citizens shall bear to the whole number male citizens twenty-one years of age in such State.

Section 3. No person shall be a Senator or Representative in Congress, or elector of President and Vice-President, or hold any office, civil or military, under the United States, or under any State, who, having the United States, or under any State, who, having previously taken an oath, as a member of Congress, or as an officer of the United States, or as a member of any State legislature ,or as an executive or judicial officer of any State, to support the Constitution of the United States, shall have engaged in insurrection or rebellion against the same, or given aid or comfort to the enemies thereof. But Congress may by a vote of two-thirds of each House, remove such disability.

Section 4. The validity of the public debt of the United States, authorized by law, including debts incurred for payment of pensions and bounties for services in suppressing insurrection or rebellion, shall not be questioned. But neither the United States nor any State shall assume or pay any debt or obligation incurred in aid of insurrection or rebellion against the United States, or any claim for the loss or emancipation of any claim for the loss or emancipation of any slave; but all such dets, obligations and claims shall be held illegal and void.

Section 5. The Congress shall have the power to enforce, by appropriate legislation, the provisions of this article.

When it comes to making things fair and square in America, the 14th Amendment is a big deal. Think of it as the rulebook for ensuring everyone gets a fair shake, regardless of where you were born or what your background is. This amendment makes it crystal clear: if you're born or naturalized in the U.S., you're an American citizen, full stop. But it doesn't stop there. It also throws a protective arm around everyone, stating that the states can't mess with your rights as a citizen or deny you the equal protection of the laws. In simpler terms, it's like saying, "Hey, everyone should be treated the same here." This was especially groundbreaking back in 1868 when it was added to the

Constitution, mainly aiming to protect the rights of newly freed slaves. However, its reach has broadened over the years, playing a key role in some major equal rights battles. Whether it's about race, gender, or other identity factors, the 14th Amendment is the backbone of arguments that demand everyone be treated equally under the law. So, it's not just a piece of history; it's a living, breathing part of our fight for fairness and justice for all.

Explained: Everyone Is Treated Equally Under the Law If you've ever heard the phrase "equal protection under the law," it's not just fancy talk. It's a principle that's meant to be at the very heart of what makes our system of government tick, thanks to the Fourteenth Amendment. This part of the Constitution says, in a nutshell, that states can't mess around with a person's rights or mess them over because of who they are or where they come from.

So, what does this look like in day-to-day life? It means that, in theory, everyone should be walking into a courtroom on equal footing. Whether you're a CEO or a janitor, the law sees you as just another person. This doesn't mean things are always perfect. Remember, laws are as good as their enforcement, and sometimes, biases sneak in. But at its core, this principle is like the north star of the legal system, guiding the way toward fairness.

Now, applying this is easier said than done. There's this balance that needs to be struck between treating everyone the same and recognizing that sometimes, to be fair, you've got to account for differences. That's where things get tricky, but it's also where our courts come into play, making judgment calls on what equality looks like in complex situations.

This equality thing extends beyond just the courtroom. It's supposed to influence how laws are written, how policies are made, and how government entities operate. For example, think about voting laws. The idea is that everyone should have an equal say in who gets elected, without unfair barriers. Or consider public education; the goal is to give every kid a fair shot at success, no matter their background.

The bottom line is, "Everyone Is Treated Equally Under the Law" sets a high bar for justice and fairness in our society. It's a goal we're always working towards, and while we've made some strides, there's always room to grow and improve. The cool part? This principle invites us all to participate, challenge unfairness, and contribute to a more equitable society. In the grand scheme of things, it's about making sure the promise of equality is real for everyone, not just a select few.

Amendment XV: Voting Rights Regardless of Race

15 **Section 1** The rights of the citizens of the United states shall not be denied or abridged by the United States or by any state on account of race, color or previous condition of servitude---

Section 2 The Congress shall have the power to enforce this article by appropriate legislation.

Imagine a time when not everyone in the United States had the right to vote, especially based on the color of their skin. That was the reality until 1870 when the 15th Amendment was added to the U.S. Constitution. This amendment marked a monumental change, stating loud and clear that the right to vote could not be denied or abridged by the United States or by any state on account of race, color, or previous condition of servitude. Basically, it was a game-changer, ensuring that African American men (women had to wait a bit longer for their turn) were officially included in the democracy party.

Why did we need this amendment, you ask? Well, after the Civil War, there were some states, particularly in the South, that were not exactly keen on the idea of former slaves having a say in elections. They came up with all sorts of barriers like literacy tests and poll taxes to keep African Americans from the polls. The 15th Amendment was supposed to put a stop to that, making it clear that voting rights were not to be messed with, no matter your skin color.

However, here's the reality check: despite this amendment, African Americans faced huge obstacles when it came to voting for nearly a century after its passage. It wasn't until the Civil Rights Movement of the 1960s and the Voting Rights Act of 1965 that the promise of the 15th Amendment was truly fulfilled across the country. That act helped to enforce the amendment, ensuring that voting rights were protected and making it illegal to use those sneaky barriers that some states were so fond of.

So, what's the big takeaway from the 15th Amendment? It's a cornerstone of our democracy, reminding us that the right to vote is fundamental and should be protected for everyone, regardless of race. It represents a crucial step toward equality and justice, but it's also a reminder of the ongoing struggle to ensure that every eligible person can cast their vote and have it counted. It's about not taking our rights for granted and recognizing the sacrifices made by those who fought so hard to ensure those rights for all.

In a nutshell, the 15th Amendment is a testament to the idea that America's democratic fabric is strongest when it's inclusive. It underscores the principle that our country's leadership should reflect its diverse population. This amendment isn't just a historical footnote; it's a living, breathing part of our democracy that continues to shape our nation's journey toward full equality. So, next time you head to the polls, remember the 15th Amendment and the role it continues to play in guaranteeing that voting right, regardless of race.

Amendment XVI: Income Tax

16 Congress shall have the power to lay and collect taxes on incomes, from whatever source derived, without appointment among the several states, and without regard to any census or enumeration.

Let's dive straight into one of the least favorite topics for many: taxes. Specifically, we're talking about the income tax, and thanks to the Sixteenth Amendment, the federal government can tax your income, no matter where it comes from. This wasn't always the case. Previously, taxes were mainly tariffs or excise taxes on goods. But as America grew, so did its financial needs, leading to the birth of the income tax.

Back in the day, the idea of the government dipping directly into people's earnings was met with resistance. It took the turn of the 20th century to see a shift in thinking, partly due to the need for more revenue and partly due to a growing sense that wealthier folks could chip in a bit more to help run the country. The Sixteenth Amendment, ratified in 1913, made it official: the U.S. government had the green light to tax incomes.

This amendment might sound straightforward, but it opened up a whole new world for government funding. Think of it as switching from a diet of solely potatoes to a full buffet. Suddenly, the government had more ways to gather resources to provide services, from building roads to funding education and defense.

Of course, not everyone was thrilled. The income tax has been a hot topic ever since its inception, sparking debates on fairness, rates, and who really bears the brunt of the tax burden. It's a key issue in many political campaigns, with promises to raise, lower, or reform income taxes being a perennial favorite among candidates.

At its core, the Sixteenth Amendment is about more than just taxes; it's about how we fund the collective project known as the United States. It reflects the balance between individual financial freedom and the shared costs of living in a society with certain expectations for services and protections.

So, the next time you're grumbling about filling out your tax return, remember that this process is rooted in a constitutional change that aimed to adjust how America pays for what it needs. It's a system that's evolved and will likely continue to evolve as we grapple with the best ways to fund our government while striving for fairness and efficiency.

In the grand scheme of the Constitution, the Sixteenth Amendment may not have the dramatic flair of the First or the controversial punch of the Second, but it plays a critical role in the functioning of modern America. It's a reminder that the Constitution isn't just about limiting government or protecting rights; it's also a tool for adapting to new challenges and ensuring the nation has the resources it needs to thrive.

Amendment XVII: Direct Election of Senators

17 The Senate of the United States shall be composed of two Senators from each state, elected by the people thereof, for six years; and each Senator shall have one vote. The electors in each state shall have the qualifications requisite for electors of the most numerous branch of the State legislators.

When vacancies happen in the representation of any State in the Senate, the exclusive authority of each State shall issue writs of election to fill such vacancies; *Provided;* That the legislature of any state may empower the executive thereof to make temporary appointments until the people fill the vacancies by election as the legislature may direct.

This amendment shall not be so construed as to affect the election or term of any Senator chosen before it becomes valid as part of the Constitution.

Before diving into the meat and potatoes of Amendment XVII, it's handy to get a picture of the "before" scenario. Initially, senators were chosen by state legislatures. This method was seen as a way to ensure that states' rights were preserved and that the federal government didn't get too big for its britches. However, as time marched on, people started scratching their heads, wondering if this was really the best way to do things. Why? Because it sometimes led to corruption and made it harder for the average Joe (or Jane) to have a say in who represented them in the Senate.

Enter Amendment XVII in 1913, which turned the tables on this process. It said, "Let's let the people vote for their senators directly." This was a huge shift towards amplifying the voice of the everyday American in their government. It meant that rather than having state legislators pick senators in smoky back rooms, the public would have the power to choose their senators directly at the ballot box. This made the process a lot more democratic and a lot less susceptible to shenanigans.

So, what drove this change? Well, the call for direct election of senators grew louder as people became more aware and fed up with the corruption and cronyism in the selection process. Stories of Senate seats being bought and sold like cattle at an auction didn't sit well with the public. The push for reform was part of a broader movement toward more democracy and transparency in the U.S. government, which included other reforms of the Progressive Era.

What this amendment essentially did was bring the Senate closer to the people it aimed to serve. Before this change, the House of Representatives was considered "the people's house" because its members were directly elected by the public. The Senate, on the other hand, seemed a bit like a private club. Amendment XVII broke down the doors of this club and made the Senate as much a part of the people's house as the House of Representatives.

In today's context, it's easy to take for granted the power to vote directly for our senators, but it's a relatively new privilege in the grand scheme of our history. This amendment reflects the ongoing American journey towards a more inclusive and participatory democracy. It's a reminder that our government isn't something far removed from our daily lives, but something we have a say in, thanks to the mechanisms like Amendment XVII that keep it accountable to us, the people.

Amendment XVIII and XXI: Prohibition and Its Repeal

18 **Section 1.** After one year from the ratification of this article the manufacture, sale, or transportation of intoxicating liquors within, the importation of intoxicating liquors within, the importation thereof into, or the exportation thereof from the United States and all territory subject to the jurisdiction thereof for beverage purposes is here-by prohibited.

Section 2. The Congress and the several States shall have concurrent power to enforce this article by appropriate legislation.

Section 3. This article shall be inoperative unless it shall have been ratified as an amendment to the Constitution by the legislatures of the several States, as provided in the Constitution within seven years from the date of the submission hereof to the States by the Congress.

21 **Section 1.** The eighteenth article of amendment to the Constitution of the United States is hereby repealed.

Section 2. The transportation or importation into any State, Territory, or Possession of the United States for delivery or use therein of intoxicating liquors, in violation of the law thereof, is hereby prohibited.

Section 3. This article shall be inoperative unless it shall have been ratified as an amendment to the Constitution by conventions in the several States, as provided in the Constitution, within seven years from the date of the submission hereof to the States by the Congress.

So, we're diving into a period in American history that might seem a bit odd today: Prohibition. This wasn't about grounding teenagers or banning video games. It was about alcohol. Yes, you read that right. The 18th Amendment to the U.S. Constitution made it illegal to make, sell, or transport alcohol. Imagine that, a whole country dry as a bone. This amendment came into effect in 1920, fueled by a movement that believed alcohol was the root of many societal problems.

But, as you can guess, not everyone was on board with this ban. In fact, it created as many problems as it aimed to solve. The rise of speakeasies, illegal bars that operated in the shadows, and bootleggers, people who smuggled alcohol, showed just how tough it is to police morality. Crime rates spiked, organized crime got a firm hold on the alcohol trade, and the government lost a bundle in tax revenue.

Enter the 21st Amendment. In 1933, it did what no other amendment has done before or since: it completely scrapped the 18th Amendment, ending national Prohibition. It's a rare example of the Constitution being used to repeal a part of itself. Why the change of heart? Well, it turns out Prohibition caused more headaches than it cured. The government realized it was fighting a losing battle and missing out on taxing legal alcohol sales.

The repeal of Prohibition wasn't just about letting folks enjoy a cold one legally again. It was a profound moment that showed the flexibility of the U.S. Constitution. It's proof that laws can evolve alongside society's values and needs, even if it means admitting previous mistakes. This period in history serves as a vivid example of how complex the relationship between law, societal norms, and individual behavior can be.

And there's an interesting sidebar here about states' rights. Even after the 21st Amendment, some states kept their own bans on alcohol for years. Mississippi didn't officially end Prohibition until 1966! It highlights how the U.S. can sometimes be a patchwork of differing laws and attitudes, emphasizing the balance between federal authority and state prerogative.

In today's discussions about substance regulation – be it alcohol, tobacco, or marijuana – the lessons from Prohibition remain relevant. It's a cautionary tale about the limits of legislation in governing personal choice and the unintended consequences that can follow.

In sum, the tale of Prohibition and its repeal teaches us valuable lessons about adaptability, the importance of a realistic approach to policy, and that sometimes, to move forward, you have to be willing to turn back. It's a fascinating story of how Americans learned that sometimes, banning something outright isn't the solution; it might just be the start of a whole new set of problems.

Amendment XIX: Women's Right to Vote

19 The right of citizens of the United States to vote shall not be denied or abridged by the United States or by any state on account of sex.

Congress shall have power to enforce this article bt appropriate legislation.

Imagine a time when half the population wasn't allowed to vote, simply because of gender. Sounds unfair, right? Well, that was the reality in the United States until the 19th Amendment was passed in 1920, granting women the right to vote. This amendment was a monumental step forward in the fight for gender equality and has had a profound impact on democracy in America.

The road to the 19th Amendment wasn't easy. It was the result of a relentless struggle by courageous women (and men) who believed in equality. Activists like Susan B. Anthony, Elizabeth Cady Stanton, and countless others dedicated their lives to this cause, organizing protests, marches, and giving speeches that would eventually change the course of history. Their efforts highlight an essential truth: securing rights and making significant changes often requires perseverance and resilience.

But why did it take so long? Well, the opposition was fierce. Many people, including some women, believed that women's suffrage would upend societal norms and the traditional family structure. Critics argued that women lacked the experience and knowledge to vote responsibly. Thankfully, the suffragettes didn't let these accusations deter them. They countered with well-reasoned arguments, public demonstrations, and civil disobedience that gradually turned the tide of public opinion in their favor.

The adoption of the 19th Amendment was not just a victory for women, but a leap forward for American democracy. It reaffirmed the Constitution's promise of equality and liberty by acknowledging that the right to vote should not be determined by gender. The amendment states, "The right of citizens of the United States to vote shall not be denied or abridged by the United States or by any State on account of sex." It's a straightforward sentence with a powerful message: equality matters.

Since its passage, the 19th Amendment has been a foundation for further advances in women's rights. It opened the door for women to become more active in politics, not just as voters but as elected officials. The increase in female participation has changed the political landscape, bringing to the forefront issues that were previously ignored or overlooked. It's a reminder that diverse perspectives lead to more balanced and fair governance.

However, the journey towards full equality continues. While the 19th Amendment granted women the right to vote, many women of color were left behind due to discriminatory practices that weren't addressed until the Voting Rights Act of 1965. This aspect of history is a stark reminder that the fight for equality is ongoing, and rights granted can never be taken for granted.

In conclusion, the 19th Amendment is more than just a historical milestone. It's a testament to the power of advocacy, the importance of equality, and the ongoing struggle for fairness and justice in America. It teaches us that change is possible, even in the face of seemingly insurmountable odds, and reminds us of our responsibility to continue working toward a more inclusive democracy.

Amendment XX: Terms of the President and Congress

20 **Section 1**. The terms of the President and the Vice President shall end at noon on the 20th day of January, and the terms of Senators and Representatives at noon on the 3rd day of January, of the years in which such terms would have ended if this article had not been ratified; and the terms of their successors shall then begin.

Section 2. The Congress shall assemble at least once in every year, and such meeting shall begin at noon on the 3d day of January, unless they shall by law appoint a different day.

Section 3. If, at the time fixed for the beginning of the term of the President, the President elect shall have died, the Vice President elect shall become President. If a President shall not have been chosen before the time fixed for the beginning of his term, or if the President elect shall have failed to qualify, then the Vice President elect shall act as President until a President shall have qualified; and the Congress may by law provide for the case wherein neither a President elect nor a Vice President shall have qualified, declaring who shall then act as President, or the manned in which one who is to act shall be selected, and such person shall act accordingly until a President or Vice President shall have qualified.

Section 4. The Congress may by law provide for the case of the death of any of the persons from whom the House of Representatives may choose a President whenever the right of choice shall have devolved upon them, and for the case of the death of any of the persons from whom the Senate may choose a Vice President whenever the right of choice shall have devolved upon them.

Section 5. Sections 1 and 2 shall take effect on the 15th day of October following the ratification of this article.

Section 6. This article shall be inoperative unless it shall have been ratified as an amendment to the Constitution by the legislatures of three-fourths of the several States within seven years from the date of its submission.

Let's dive into the Twentieth Amendment, a piece of constitutional text that's all about timing. In essence, this amendment helps keep our political train running on schedule, setting clear dates for the start and end of terms for the President, Vice President, and members of Congress. It might not sound like the stuff of dramatic movie plots, but these details matter. Before this amendment was introduced in 1933, there was quite a bit of a lag between election day and when these officials actually kicked off their tenures—think of it as a "lame-duck" period. This could get pretty awkward, especially if a lot of new folks were stepping in.

For the President and Vice President, the amendment says their terms end at noon on January 20, and that's when the next ones start. For Congress, their terms wrap up and start on January 3. This might seem like just calendar notes, but it's about making sure our government doesn't lose time when it's supposed to be getting things done. Before this amendment, there was a much longer wait until March for these changes to take place. You can imagine how, in times of crisis, a delay like that could really throw a wrench in things.

Another key piece of the Twentieth Amendment is about what happens if the President-elect can't take office—whether because of passing away, not qualifying, or other reasons. It allows Congress to step in and decide who acts as President until the situation can be sorted out. This part is like having a backup plan for your backup plan, ensuring the leadership of the country is never in limbo.

So, why did we need this "Lame-Duck Amendment"? Back in the day, long before we had cars zooming around and the internet keeping us connected, it made sense to wait months after an election to get everyone to the capital. But as technology and transportation got better, that long wait wasn't just unnecessary; it could be downright risky, leaving the country hanging in the balance during tough times.

In wrapping up, the Twentieth Amendment is a prime example of the Constitution evolving with the times. It's about making sure the transition of power is smooth, timely, and leaves no room for unnecessary delays. Just like updating your phone keeps it running smoothly, amendments like these keep our government up to speed. So next time January rolls around, and you hear talk of Inauguration Day, you'll know the Twentieth Amendment is doing its job, making sure our leaders are ready to roll when we need them.

Amendment XXII: Limit on Presidential Terms

22 **Section 1.** No person shall be elected to the office of the President more than twice, and no person who has held the office of President, or acted as President, for more than two years of a term to which some other person was elected President shall be elected to the office of President more than once. But this article shall not apply to any person holding the office of President when this Article was proposed by Congress, and shall not prevent any person who may be holding the office of President, or acting as President, during the term within which this Article becomes operative from holding the office of President or acting as President during the remainder of such term.

Section 2. This article shall be inoperative unless it shall have ratified as an amendment to the Constitution by the legislatures of three-fourths of the several States within even years from the date of its submission to the State by the Congress.

Let's dive into the 22nd Amendment, a rule that puts a cap on how long someone can be President of the United States. Before this amendment came into play, a President could serve as many terms as they were elected to. This changed after Franklin D. Roosevelt was elected for a fourth term, which sparked a debate about the risks of one person holding this much power for too long. So, in 1951, the 22nd Amendment was added to the Constitution, making it clear that a President can only be elected to two terms, which amounts to eight years in total.

The heart of this amendment is about maintaining a balance of power and ensuring that no single individual can hold the presidency for an indefinite period. It's like saying, "Hey, being President is a huge deal, but let's give other people a shot at leading, too." This prevents any President from gaining too much control over the government and helps keep our democracy fresh and dynamic.

There's a bit more to it, though. If a Vice President or anyone else steps in as President and serves more than two years of someone else's term, they can only be elected President once. The idea here is to make sure no one edges around the system to stay in power for longer than they should. It's all about keeping things fair and not letting the presidency turn into a longer gig than it was meant to be.

This amendment shows the beauty of the American system where checks and balances are key. It reminds us that in a democracy, power is supposed to be in rotation, not stuck in a loop. By setting a limit on the presidency, it keeps the spirit of democracy alive, making sure that new ideas and perspectives get a chance to lead the country forward.

So, the 22nd Amendment is more than just a rule about term limits; it's a safeguard for our democracy. It ensures that no single person can become too powerful and encourages a healthy turnover in leadership. This keeps our democracy vibrant, competitive, and most importantly, fair.

Amendment XXIII: Voting Rights for residents of Washington D.C.

23 **Section 1** The District constituting the seat of Government of the United States shall appoint in such manner as Congress may direct:

A number of electors of President and Vice President equal to the whole number of Senators and Representatives in Congress to which the District would be entitled if it were a State, but in no event more than the least populace State; they shall be in addition to those appointed by the States, but they shall be considered, for the purposes of the election of President and Vice President , to be electors appointed by a State; and they shall meet in the district and preform such duties as provided by the twelfth article of amendment.

Section 2 The Congress shall have the power to enforce this article by appropriate legislation.

Imagine living in the heart of the United States, surrounded by symbols of democracy, yet not having a say in electing the president of your country. Sounds unfair, right? Before the 23rd Amendment was ratified in 1961, that was the reality for residents of Washington D.C. They could serve in the military, pay federal taxes, and contribute to the nation in every way, but when it came to presidential elections, they had no voice. This amendment changed that by granting them the right to vote for the president and vice president.

Here's how it works: the Amendment gives D.C. a number of electors in the Electoral College equal to the smallest state, regardless of its population. This means D.C. residents can now have their say on who leads the nation, bringing them closer to the rights enjoyed by citizens in the fifty states. It was a milestone in American democracy, expanding the franchise and making the concept of no taxation without representation a bit more real for folks living in the nation's capital.

But it's not all sunshine and roses. While the 23rd Amendment granted presidential voting rights, D.C. still doesn't have voting representation in Congress. That means residents can vote for the president but lack a voice in creating the very laws they live under. It's a bit like being invited to the party but not being allowed to weigh in on the playlist or the menu. This remains a contentious issue, with many arguing for further changes to ensure full representation for D.C. residents.

Understanding the 23rd Amendment shines a light on broader issues of representation and voting rights in the U.S. It's a reminder that democracy is a work in progress, constantly evolving to include more voices in the process. The fight for representation in Washington D.C. is an ongoing chapter in the larger story of American democracy, highlighting the importance of every citizen's right to vote and be heard.

In a nutshell, the 23rd Amendment was a significant step forward in addressing a centuries-old oversight in American democracy, but it also opened the door to further debates about representation for D.C. residents. It's a perfect example of how amendments are not just historical footnotes but alive, influencing current discussions about fairness and equality in our democracy. For people living in the heart of the U.S., it represents a partial victory in their long journey towards full participation in American political life.

Amendment XXIV: Abolition of Poll Taxes

24 **Section 1** The right of citizens of the United States to vote in any primary or other election for President or Vice President; for electors for President or Vice President, or for Senator or Representative in

Congress, shall not be denied or abridged by the United States or any State by reason of failure to pay poll tax pr other tax.

Section 2 The Congress shall have the power to enforce this article by appropriate legislation.

Imagine walking into your local polling station, ready to cast your vote for the next president, only to be met with a fee to access the voting booth. Sounds unfair, right? Well, that was the reality for many Americans before the 24th Amendment came into play. The 24th Amendment, ratified in 1964, put an end to poll taxes in federal elections, a practice that had been used to prevent low-income individuals, particularly African Americans in the South, from exercising their right to vote.

Poll taxes were essentially a pay-to-vote scheme. States imposed these taxes as part of the Jim Crow laws, designed to enforce racial segregation and disenfranchisement. Because many African Americans and poor white voters couldn't afford to pay the tax, they were effectively barred from participating in democracy. The 24th Amendment abolished this barrier, reinforcing that the right to vote shouldn't be dependent on a person's financial situation.

The amendment reads, quite simply, "The right of citizens of the United States to vote in any primary or other election for President or Vice President, for electors for President or Vice President, or for Senator or Representative in Congress, shall not be denied or abridged by the United States or any State by reason of failure to pay any poll tax or other tax." This was a crucial step forward in ensuring that all citizens, regardless of their economic status, had a voice in their government.

While the 24th Amendment addressed federal elections, some states continued to require poll taxes for state and local elections. It wasn't until the Supreme Court case of Harper v. Virginia State Board of Elections in 1966 that the practice was deemed unconstitutional in state elections as well. The ruling emphasized that wealth or payment of any fee should not limit a citizen's right to vote.

The abolition of poll taxes by the 24th Amendment marked a pivotal moment in the civil rights movement, dismantling yet another Jim Crow law and moving the United States closer to equality for all its citizens. It underscored the principle that democracy works best when it's accessible to everyone. Through this amendment, the nation took a significant step towards eliminating economic barriers to voting, ensuring that every voice could be heard, loud and clear, in the halls of power.

Amendment XXV: Presidential Disability and Succession

25 **Section 1**. In case of the removal of the President from office or of his death or resignation, the Vice President shall become President.

Section 2. Whenever there is a vacancy in the office of the Vice President, the President shall nominate a Vice President who shall take office upon confirmation by a majority vote of both House of Congress.

Section 3. Whenever the President transmits to the President pro tempore of the Senate and the Speaker of the House of Representatives his written declaration that he is unable to discharge the powers and duties of his office, and until he transmits to them a written declaration to the contrary, such powers and duties shall be discharged by the Vice President as Acting President.

Section 4. Whenever the Vice President and a majority of either the principal officers of the executive departments or of such other body as Congress may by law provide, transmit to the President pro tempore of the Senate and the Speaker of the House of Representatives their written declaration that the President is unable to discharge the powers and duties of his office, the Vice President shall immediately assume the powers and duties of the office as Acting President.

Thereafter, when the President transmits to the President pro tempore of the Senate and the Speaker of the House of Representatives his written declaration that no inability exists, he shall resume the powers and duties of his office unless the Vice President and a majority of either the principal officers of the executive department or of such other body as Congress may by law provide, transmit within four days to the President pro tempore of the Senate and the Speaker of the House of Representatives his written declaration that no inability exists, he shall resume the powers and duties of his office unless the Vice President and a majority of either the principal officers of the executive department or of such other body as Congress may by law provide, transmit within four days to the President pro tempore of the Senate and the Speaker of the House of Representatives their written declaration that the President is unable to discharge the powers and duties of his office. There-upon Congress shall decide the issue, assembling within forty-eight hours for that purpose if not in session. If the Congress, within twenty-one days after receipt of the latter written declaration, or, if Congress is not in session, within twenty-one days after Congress is required to assemble, determines by two-thirds vote of both Houses that the President is unable to discharge the powers and duties of his office, the Vice President shall continue to discharge the same as Acting President; otherwise, the President shall resume the powers and duties of his office.

Imagine running a relay race where if the lead runner trips, someone else can seamlessly take over and keep racing towards the finish line. The 25th Amendment to the U.S. Constitution provides a similar "just in case" plan for the Presidency. It's all about what happens if a President can't do the job, either because of illness or if there's a need to fill the Vice President's spot. Let's break it down into simpler terms.

First off, before this amendment was added in 1967, there wasn't a clear, spelled-out plan for what to do if the President were incapacitated. The 25th Amendment cleared up any guesswork. It consists of four sections, each designed to handle a different "what if" scenario involving the President and Vice President.

The first section is pretty straightforward: if the President dies or steps down, the Vice President becomes President. Simple, right? This part was more or less understood even before this amendment, but it's always good to have things in writing.

Section two tackles the issue of what to do if there's a vacancy in the Vice Presidency. According to the amendment, the President gets to pick a new Vice President, but this choice must be approved by both houses of Congress. This ensures that the process is not just a one-person decision but involves key players in our government.

Moving on to section three, we find a provision for a President who knows they're going to be incapacitated, maybe for a surgery or an illness they're aware of in advance. In these situations, the President can write to the House Speaker and the Senate's temporary President to say, "Hey, my Vice President is in charge until I'm back in the saddle." This keeps the executive branch running smoothly even when the President is temporarily out of commission.

The fourth section is the most complex: it's for when the President might be unable to recognize their own incapacity. If the Vice President and a majority of either the Cabinet or another body appointed by Congress believe the President can't do the job, they can write to Congress saying the Vice President should step in as acting President. This situation requires a delicate balance because it deals with a potentially unwilling or unaware President, offering a solution that respects the office's dignity while ensuring the country's leadership remains effective and responsive.

The 25th Amendment shows the importance of planning for every contingency, even in the highest office in the land. In providing clear guidelines for presidential disability and succession, it's like the Constitution's way of saying, "Let's keep the show going, no matter what happens." It's about stability, ensuring there's always someone at the helm, guiding the United States forward.

Amendment XXVI: Voting Age Set to 18 Years

26 **Section 1** The right of citizens of the United States who are eighteen years of age or older, to vote shall not be denied or abridged by the United States or any State on account of age.

Section 2 The Congress shall have power to enforce this article by appropriate legislation.

Imagine being 18, at an age where you can be called upon to serve your country, but you can't vote for the president or even your local mayor. That was the reality before the 26th Amendment came along. This part of our Constitution journey dives into the amendment that lowered the voting age from 21 to 18. It was a significant change that echoed the nation's sentiments during a turbulent period. Let's break it down to understand why it matters to everyone, whether you're just hitting adulthood or you've been voting for decades.

Back in the late 60s and early 70s, the United States was in the thick of the Vietnam War. Young people nationwide were being drafted to fight in a war, yet they had no say in the elections. "Old enough to fight, old enough to vote" became a rallying cry. It highlighted a glaring inconsistency in the rights of young adults. The movement gained momentum, and it wasn't long before politicians took notice. The change wasn't just about fairness; it was about acknowledging the maturity and the capabilities of younger adults.

So, in 1971, Congress passed the 26th Amendment, and it was ratified in record time. States quickly jumped on board, understanding the importance of giving younger Americans a voice. This amendment is a testament to the idea that if society expects you to take on adult responsibilities, you should also enjoy adult privileges, such as voting. It recognized 18-year-olds as adults in not just fighting for their country but in contributing to its democratic decisions.

The impact of this amendment goes beyond just allowing younger people to vote. It's been a powerful tool for energizing political movements and encouraging civic engagement among the youth. Every election cycle, we see efforts on college campuses and high schools geared towards getting young people to register and vote. It's a right that was fought for, a reminder of the power of advocacy and the importance of having a say in how our country is run.

In sum, the 26th Amendment is a significant milestone in the journey towards extending liberty and justice for all. Lowering the voting age to 18 has opened up the democratic process, ensuring that younger voices are heard and valued. It's a meaningful affirmation that in a democracy, the right to vote isn't just a privilege—it's a powerful tool for change, accessible to all adults, regardless of age.

Amendment XXVII: Congressional Pay Limitations

27 No law, varying the compensation for the services of the Senators and Representatives, shall take effect, until an election of representatives shall have intervened.

Let's dive into the last stop on our journey through the amendments, shall we? The Twenty-Seventh Amendment is kind of the 'slow and steady wins the race' of the Constitution. It's about money, but not in the way you might think. This amendment makes sure that if Congress decides to change the amount they're paid, that change doesn't kick in until after the next election of Representatives.

This means they can't just give themselves a raise whenever they feel like it; they have to wait it out and see if they get re-elected first.

Why does this matter? It's all about accountability. If lawmakers want to up their salaries, they have to face the music and make sure their constituents are okay with it come election time. It's a check on power that makes sure those in charge stay connected with the folks they represent. They can't just bloat the government budget on their salaries without thinking about the repercussions. It encourages a bit of humility and foresight, qualities that are, frankly, pretty crucial in our leaders.

Now, here's a fun fact: this amendment holds the record for the longest ratification process in history. Proposed in 1789 and not ratified until 1992, it's the constitutional equivalent of a fine wine taking its sweet time to mature. It's a stark reminder that sometimes, change in a democracy takes a bit more time than you'd expect.

So, what's the big takeaway from Amendment XXVII? It's a safeguard, pure and simple. In a system that's all about balance and checks, this amendment puts the power back where it belongs- with the people. Lawmakers have got to think twice before giving themselves a pay bump, ensuring they remain servants of the public, not the other way round.

As we wrap up our exploration of the amendments, the XXVII stands as a testament to the enduring nature of the U.S. Constitution. It's a lasting promise that our government remains of the people, by the people, for the people, even when it comes to the nitty-gritty of congressional paychecks.

Chapter 4:
Understanding the Amendments
Through Modern Issues

In diving into Chapter 4, we're bridging the gap between the inked words of the past and the digital buzz of the present, tackling how centuries-old amendments play out on today's high-tech stage. First up, we've got free speech in the digital age - think tweets, posts, and all that jazz. It's no longer just about shouting your thoughts on a street corner; it's about the global audience you can reach with the click of a button. Then, we slide into the ever-polarizing world of gun rights and regulation debates. It's a tightrope walk between securing personal freedoms and ensuring public safety, with each side packing a punch in arguments. And don't forget about privacy and surveillance - where the line blurs between keeping countries safe and keeping personal lives private. It's a whole new ballgame with technology that the Founding Fathers couldn't have dreamed of. So, let's peel back the layers of history and see how the timeless principles of the Constitution hold up under the unforgiving lights of the 21st century.

Free Speech in the Digital Age

In today's world, the concept of free speech has evolved far beyond what the Founding Fathers might have imagined, especially with the advent of the digital age. The First Amendment, a cornerstone of American democracy, protects the right to free speech, among other freedoms. Yet, as we navigate through the vast and sometimes murky waters of the internet, applying this 18th-century principle to 21st-century technology proves to be a complex task.

The internet has effectively democratized information, giving a platform to voices that, in the past, might have been silenced or overlooked. This means anyone with access to the internet can share their thoughts, opinions, and beliefs worldwide. While this represents an unprecedented expansion of the marketplace of ideas, it also introduces challenges. These include issues around hate speech, misinformation, and the silencing of voices through digital harassment.

One major question is how free speech rights apply on social media platforms, which have become the modern public square. These platforms, while private companies, hold significant power over public discourse, leading to debates about their responsibilities in regulating content. Should they act as arbiters of truth, or should they remain neutral, allowing all voices to be heard, regardless of the potential harm?

Moreover, the digital age has brought about concerns regarding anonymity online. Anonymity can protect vulnerable individuals, enabling them to express controversial opinions without fear of retribution. However, it can also shield those who spread hate or engage in cyberbullying. Finding the balance between protecting free speech and preventing harm has become a pressing issue for societies worldwide.

Another aspect to consider is the role of governments in regulating the internet. In efforts to control misinformation and hate speech, some governments have imposed regulations that can infringe on free speech. This raises important questions about censorship and the potential for government overreach under the guise of protecting public order or national security.

The challenge lies in crafting laws and regulations that address these concerns without stifling innovation or curbing the fundamental right to free speech. It's a delicate balancing act, requiring a nuanced understanding of both the technical aspects of the digital world and the legal principles of free expression.

For us, as users of digital platforms, it involves understanding the power of our words and the impact they can have in this interconnected world. It's about exercising our rights responsibly and critically evaluating the information we consume and share. Digital literacy becomes key in discerning credible sources from misinformation.

Engaging in thoughtful discussions about the limits of free speech, the responsibilities of digital platforms, and the role of government in this digital era is crucial. It's not just a matter for policymakers and tech companies; it involves all of us. After all, the vibrant exchange of ideas and information is a hallmark of a healthy democracy.

As we move forward, it's important to remember that the principles of free speech and freedom of expression are foundational to any free society. The digital age presents new challenges, but it also offers new opportunities to ensure these principles are preserved and adapted effectively for future generations.

In conclusion, navigating free speech in the digital age is complex, requiring a careful balance between protecting individual rights and addressing the potential harms of unfettered expression. As technology continues to evolve, so too will our understanding and application of these fundamental freedoms. By staying informed and engaged, we can all contribute to shaping a digital landscape that upholds the values of democracy and free expression.

Gun Rights and Regulation Debates

The Second Amendment to the U.S. Constitution grants Americans the right to bear arms but hasn't made the debates around gun rights and regulation any simpler. This conversation has layers, much like an onion, and peeling each layer reveals more complexity and passionate viewpoints. The core of the debate centers on how we balance individual rights with public safety, a question as old as the Constitution itself.

At its heart, the Second Amendment was about ensuring a form of security. Some interpret this as the right for individuals to own and carry guns. Others see it as a collective right, emphasizing a well-regulated militia's importance for security. Over time, the pendulum of public opinion and legal interpretation has swung between these perspectives, influenced by changing social conditions and landmark Supreme Court decisions.

One significant case that shaped our modern understanding of gun rights is *District of Columbia v. Heller* (2008). This case underscored the individual's right to own a gun for personal use, striking down a Washington D.C. law that effectively banned handguns in the home. The decision was groundbreaking, yet, it also recognized that the right to bear arms is not absolute. Regulations like background checks, and prohibitions on gun ownership by felons, were deemed consistent with the Second Amendment.

Despite *Heller*, or perhaps because of it, the debate over gun control has intensified. Calls for more stringent regulations increase in the wake of mass shootings, with advocates pushing for measures like universal background checks, restrictions on high-capacity magazines, and bans on certain assault-style weapons. Opponents of such measures argue that they infringe on individual freedoms and won't effectively address the root causes of gun violence.

This debate isn't just about interpreting a historical document. It's about how we live today and the kind of society we want to be. Do stricter gun laws save lives? Or do they unduly restrict personal freedom? These questions aren't easy, and opinions vary widely across the American political and geographical landscape.

A notable aspect of the gun rights debate is its cultural significance. In many parts of the United States, gun ownership is deeply interwoven with cultural identity, symbolizing values such as independence, self-reliance, and individual rights. This cultural dimension adds a layer of complexity to the debate, making consensus even harder to achieve.

Moreover, technological advancements have introduced new variables into the gun control equation. The emergence of 3D-printed firearms and so-called "ghost guns" (guns assembled from parts without serial numbers) poses challenges for regulation and law enforcement, indicating that the debate will continue to evolve with technology.

At its core, the discussion about gun rights and regulation debates is about finding a balance between freedom and safety. It's a delicate balancing act, requiring careful consideration of historical precedents, legal interpretations, social needs, and technological advancements. As society changes, so too will the contours of this debate, reflecting the ever-evolving relationship between Americans and their guns.

Ultimately, comprehending the Second Amendment in the 21st century demands an understanding that it's not just about the letter of the law but about its spirit—how it shapes our society, influences our culture, and reflects our values. The debates around gun rights and regulation are, at their heart, about how we interpret freedom, responsibility, and security in a changing world. Engaging in these discussions, regardless of where you stand, is part of what it means to be an informed and active participant in American democracy.

As we move forward, it's crucial to approach these debates with an open mind and a willingness to listen. The answers may not be simple, but through respectful dialogue and thoughtful consideration, progress is possible. Understanding the intricacies of gun rights and regulations is not just about guns—it's about defining the kind of country we want to live in.

Privacy and Surveillance in the 21st Century

In today's world, the words 'privacy' and 'surveillance' carry more weight than ever. It's not just about someone possibly eavesdropping on your conversation anymore, but how our digital fingerprints, from text messages to web searches, are tracked, stored, and analyzed. Understanding the Fourth Amendment—our shield against unreasonable searches and seizures—is crucial in navigating this landscape. The Amendment was designed to protect your papers and effects from unwarranted government eyes, a concept that's constantly evolving with technology.

Consider the world we live in: smartphones, smart homes, online banking, social media, and the list goes on. Each platform collects data, revealing intimate details of our lives. Here's where the Fourth Amendment conversation gets tricky. The line between protecting national security and preserving individual privacy has become blurred. How do we balance these scales? It's a question that's been thrust upon courts and lawmakers in the digital age.

High-profile cases and government programs have brought the tension between surveillance for security and the right to privacy into sharp relief. For instance, the Edward Snowden revelations in 2013 exposed the vast extent of government surveillance programs, sparking global debate. The key question isn't just about what is legal, but what should be legal when it comes to privacy in a digital era.

Moreover, the role of tech companies in this equation cannot be overstated. They collect an immense volume of data, governed by terms and conditions that few people read thoroughly, if at all. This data can be requested by governments or leaked to malicious actors, leading to significant privacy breaches. The involvement of these corporations adds another layer of complexity to privacy rights and raises questions about corporate responsibility alongside governmental oversight.

Legislation, like the USA PATRIOT Act, has sought to address these challenges, but it's a tightrope walk. These laws expand the government's surveillance capabilities in an effort to combat terrorism, yet they also raise concerns about overreach into personal privacy. Legal battles and public discourse around these acts underscore the ongoing struggle to find a balance.

It's important for individuals to stay informed about their digital rights and the measures they can take to protect their privacy, such as using encryption and understanding the privacy policies of the platforms they use. However, individual actions alone can't address the broader issues at hand. Public advocacy and informed debate are essential in shaping policies that govern surveillance and privacy.

Ultimately, the conversation about privacy and surveillance in the 21st century is an evolving one. It touches on fundamental questions about the relationship between individuals, the state, and corporations in a digital world. As technology advances, so too must our understanding of what it means to be free from unreasonable searches and seizures. It's a topic that affects us all, demanding our attention and engagement.

Chapter 5:
How to Exercise Your Rights

Now that we've explored the roots and branches of the U.S. Constitution and its amendments, let's roll up our sleeves and dive into how you can actively exercise these rights you're armed with. It's one thing to know your rights on paper, but it's another to put them into action in your day-to-day life. Engaging in civic duties is a solid starting point. Whether it means voting during elections to make your voice heard, serving on a jury to participate in the judicial process, or simply understanding the responsibilities that come with your rights, it's your first step towards an active civic life. Protecting your rights is crucial too. Know that you have the power to stand up if your rights are ever infringed upon. This may involve everything from knowing when to speak up during a traffic stop to understanding the ramifications of postings on social media. Finally, getting involved in local governance can make a world of difference in exercising your rights. From attending town hall meetings to participating in local community groups, you have the opportunity to influence decisions that affect your everyday life. Remember, your involvement in these areas strengthens not only your understanding of your rights but also the very fabric of our democracy.

Engaging in Civic Duties

When it comes to being an active participant in our democracy, engaging in civic duties is a cornerstone. It's not just about staying informed or knowing what rights the Constitution guarantees you; it's about taking action and being a part of the decision-making process. Voting is perhaps the most well-known civic duty, and it's a powerful way to have your voice heard. But there's a lot more to civic engagement than marking a ballot every couple of years. Let's break down what it means to truly engage with your civic duties.

First off, serving on a jury is a responsibility a lot of folks might not think too much about until they receive that summons in the mail. But here's the thing, it's a direct way to contribute to justice being served in your community. It's about ensuring that a peer's fate is carefully considered by a group of their fellow citizens, not just left in the hands of a single judge. Participating in the judiciary process in this way is a fundamental aspect of our rights under the Constitution, emphasizing the importance of fair trials and due process.

Then there's the role of staying informed. It might sound simple, but in today's world with news flying at us from a million different directions, it's more challenging and necessary than ever. Understanding the issues, knowing where candidates stand on those issues, and grasping the implications of local and national policies requires effort. But it's this very effort that ensures our democracy is vibrant and responsive. We can't make informed decisions if we're not, well, informed.

Moreover, engaging in civic duties extends beyond formal processes like voting or jury duty; it involves community participation. This could mean attending town hall meetings, joining local boards, or participating in public demonstrations for causes you believe in. It's about finding your voice in the civic conversation and helping shape the community around you. These actions might seem small in isolation but collectively, they contribute to the democratic dialogue and can lead to significant changes.

Lastly, don't forget about the role of dialogue and respect in civic engagement. In a time when political discourse can become incredibly divided, it's crucial to remember the value of understanding different perspectives. Engaging with people whose views differ from yours, in a respectful and constructive manner, strengthens the fabric of our democracy. It's through these exchanges that we can find common ground and work towards solutions that benefit everyone.

So there you have it, engaging in civic duties is multifaceted; it's about being an active participant in the democracy that shapes our lives. It goes beyond simply knowing your rights and extends into how you use them to contribute to the community and the country at large. Remember, every action, no matter how small it may seem, counts in keeping our democratic system strong and vibrant.

Protecting Your Rights

So, you're clued up on the basics of the Constitution and the Bill of Rights. That's great! But understanding your rights is just the beginning. Keeping those rights safe and sound? That's where the real challenge kicks in. It's like knowing the rules of the road doesn't automatically make you a good driver. You've got to put those rules into practice, stay alert, and sometimes, take action to protect yourself and others.

First up, awareness is key. You can't protect what you don't know you have. Make it your business to stay informed. Read up on current events, listen to varied perspectives, and keep an eye out for any laws or policies that might affect your rights. It's like being on your own personal security detail, but instead of safeguarding a VIP, you're looking out for your constitutional rights.

Now, let's talk action. Voting isn't just a right; it's a powerhouse tool for safeguarding your freedoms. By voting, you have a say in who makes the laws and how those laws are made. It's your chance to support candidates and policies that back your views on the rights you cherish most. Not to mention, being an active participant in local governance—from town hall meetings to community boards—puts you in the driver's seat when it comes to local policy decisions that could affect your rights.

But what if you come across a situation where your rights are being challenged? That's where knowing how to advocate for yourself comes in handy. Whether it's freedom of speech, the right to privacy, or any other right, being able to articulate what's at stake and seeking legal advice when necessary can make all the difference. Sometimes you might need to take legal action to protect your rights, and that's okay. The legal system exists, in part, for that very purpose.

Education plays a massive role, too. Sharing your knowledge about rights with friends, family, and your community doesn't just help you; it strengthens the fabric of our democracy. The more people know about their rights, the tougher it becomes for those rights to be eroded. It's like a neighborhood watch program for constitutional rights. Everyone looks out for each other, making it harder for injustices to go unchallenged.

Lastly, don't underestimate the power of your voice. Writing to your representatives, participating in peaceful protests, and signing petitions are all ways to make your voice heard. These actions remind those in power that they are accountable to the people. In a democracy, there's strength in numbers, and when voices come together for a common cause, they're hard to ignore.

Protecting your rights isn't a one-time deal; it's a continuous commitment. But don't worry, you're not in it alone. When you stand up for your rights, you stand with countless others who share your commitment to liberty and justice. It's a journey worth taking, so let's keep those rights safe, together.

Getting Involved in Local Governance

Now, let's talk about getting your feet wet in local governance. It's the closest layer of government to us, yet so many of us overlook its significance. Local governance is where the rubber meets the road - it's where policies and decisions have a direct impact on our daily lives, from the potholes that need filling on our streets to the funding of our schools. But here's the kicker: as much as these issues affect us, involvement in local governance remains remarkably low. It's time to change that tune.

First off, understanding how your town or city functions is crucial. Each local government has its own set of rules and structures, from city councils to school boards. These bodies make decisions on everything affecting your immediate environment. And guess what? They want to hear from you. Public comments at these meetings aren't just a formality. They can influence decisions. If speaking up in meetings isn't your cup of tea, many councils and boards have committees you can join to work on specific issues, be it urban planning, education, or public safety.

Now, for those itching to dive deeper, running for a local office could be your calling. It's a powerful way to effect change. You don't have to start big. School boards, zoning commissions, and local councils are great places to start. The beauty of local offices is that they're more accessible than you might think. Plus, serving your community in this way can be incredibly rewarding.

But let's not forget the power of volunteering. Local governments often rely on volunteers for various initiatives, from environmental projects to community events. Volunteering not only allows you to contribute directly to your community's welfare but also gives you a behind-the-scenes look at how decisions are made and how projects are implemented.

In conclusion, getting involved in local governance is a fantastic avenue to exercise your rights and influence the place you call home. Whether it's through attending meetings, serving on committees, running for office, or volunteering, your participation can drive real change. Remember, local governance works best when it includes a diverse range of voices - yours included. It's all about taking that first step.

Chapter 6:
The Role of the Supreme Court in Interpreting the Constitution

Now that we've toured through the amendments and touched on modern issues, let's dive into the big leagues where nine justices hold the power to interpret the very fabric of American law - the Supreme Court. This isn't just about a group of folks in robes making decisions on a whim. It's about a crucial process that tests the elasticity of the U.S. Constitution, stretching it to cover issues the Founding Fathers could hardly have imagined. Picture the Constitution as the rule book for the nation. Well, the Supreme Court acts like the ultimate referee, calling the shots on how those rules apply today. From battles over free speech to the rights of the accused, these justices dissect every word of the Constitution to ensure it remains a living, breathing document that grows with the nation. Each case they decide on is like adding another layer to the story of America, shaping the country's legal landscape and, by extension, the lives of its people. So, whether it's deciding if your phone can be searched without a warrant or if states can put limits on gun ownership, the Supreme Court's role in interpreting the Constitution is vital, constantly defining and redefining what those age-old texts mean for every American.

Key Cases That Have Shaped Our Understanding of the Amendments

The role of the Supreme Court in interpreting the Constitution cannot be overstated. Through various cases, they've profoundly shaped our understanding of its amendments. Let's dive into some key cases that stand out for their impact.

Starting with the First Amendment, the case of **Brandenburg v. Ohio** in 1969 set a precedent for the ability to freely express oneself. The Court's ruling emphasized that speech could only be restricted if it's likely to incite lawless action, creating a robust defense for free speech.

Then there's the Second Amendment, often discussed in the context of gun rights. **District of Columbia v. Heller** in 2008 was a landmark decision here. The Court ruled that individuals have a right to possess firearms for lawful purposes, such as self-defense within the home, which clarified the amendment's scope.

When talking about the Fourth Amendment and the right to privacy, **Mapp v. Ohio** in 1961 was a game-changer. It extended the exclusionary rule to the states, meaning evidence obtained in violation of the Fourth Amendment could not be admitted in court.

The Fifth Amendment's protection against self-incrimination was underscored by the **Miranda v. Arizona** case in 1966. The ruling mandated that detained criminal suspects be informed of their rights, including the right to an attorney and the right to remain silent, before questioning.

Another significant Fifth Amendment case, **Kelo v. City of New London** in 2005, redefined the concept of public use. It stated that the government could seize private property for economic development purposes under the amendment's Takings Clause, which sparked a huge debate and led many states to revise their laws.

The Sixth Amendment ensures the right to a fair trial, which was profoundly impacted by **Gideon v. Wainwright** in 1963. This case guaranteed the right to an attorney for those who could not afford one, emphasizing the importance of legal representation in the pursuit of justice.

Moving to the Eighth Amendment's protection against excessive bails, fines, and cruel and unusual punishment, **Furman v. Georgia** in 1972 temporarily halted capital punishment in the United States. It prompted a reevaluation of death penalty procedures, leading many states to revise their laws.

The Fourteenth Amendment is a cornerstone for civil rights, and **Brown v. Board of Education** in 1954 used it to declare state laws establishing segregated schools unconstitutional. This decision was pivotal in the fight against racial segregation in America.

Regarding voting rights under the Fifteenth Amendment, **Shelby County v. Holder** in 2013 reshaped the enforcement of the Voting Rights Act. The Court's decision effectively struck down a key provision that required certain states to obtain federal permission before changing voting laws, arguing it was based on outdated information.

The Nineteenth Amendment granted women the right to vote, but it wasn't a Supreme Court case that tested its bounds; it was the relentless activism and advocacy of women's rights activists that cemented its place in American society.

For the Twenty-fourth Amendment, which prohibits poll taxes in federal elections, **Harper v. Virginia State Board of Elections** in 1966 extended this prohibition to state elections as well, reinforcing that wealth should not influence one's ability to vote.

The **Obergefell v. Hodges** decision in 2015 highlighted the Fourteenth Amendment's due process and equal protection clauses by guaranteeing the right to marry to same-sex couples. This landmark case ensured that marriage rights could not be denied based on gender.

Lastly, the importance of the Twenty-sixth Amendment, which lowered the voting age to 18, was affirmed in cases not by contested in the Supreme Court but through legislative actions prompted by societal changes and activism during the Vietnam War era.

These cases represent just a handful of the Supreme Court decisions that have played a significant role in defining and clarifying the rights and freedoms we hold dear. Each case serves as a reminder of the Constitution's living nature and the crucial role the judicial system plays in interpreting its words.

In conclusion, the Supreme Court's interpretations of the Constitution have not only clarified the meaning of its amendments but have also adapted them to the evolving societal norms, technologies, and values. These cases show the dynamic between law and society, proving the Constitution to be a living document that continues to guide and protect the American people.

Chapter 7: The process of Amending the Constitution -

Think of the U.S. Constitution as a sturdy yet flexible backbone of our nation, strong enough to hold us together but flexible enough to bend with the times. Amending it, though, is no simple task, and that's by design. The framers set it up this way to ensure that changes reflect a broad consensus rather than fleeting popular opinions. So, how does an idea scribbled on a napkin at a coffee shop become a part of this venerable document? It's a two-stage rocket: proposal and ratification.

First up, proposal. An amendment can be proposed in two ways. Congress, with a two-thirds majority in both the House of Representatives and the Senate, can vote to propose an amendment. Or, if two-thirds of the state legislatures demand it, a convention can be called to propose new amendments, a path less traveled in our history.

Next is ratification. Once proposed, the amendment needs to be ratified, or approved, by three-fourths of the state legislatures or conventions in three-fourths of the states. It's a steep hill to climb, ensuring that only those amendments with widespread support make the cut.

This process underscores the beauty of our system: it's built to adapt and evolve. While it's tough to amend the Constitution, it's not impossible. It's been done twenty-seven times, after all. Each amendment is a testament to the ability of the American people to refine and improve their government, ensuring it serves its purpose for generations to come. So next time you hear about an amendment in the works, you'll know just what hurdles it has to clear on its way to becoming part of the grand experiment that is the United states.

How New Amendments Are Made

So, you're curious about how a new amendment gets etched into the U.S. Constitution? It's not magic, it's a process—and quite the journey for any idea looking to become part of the nation's most important document. Think of it as a game where only the strongest contenders reach the finish line, requiring a blend of widespread support and timely action.

Initially, an amendment must be proposed. This can happen one of two ways. The most common route is through Congress, where both the Senate and the House of Representatives must agree. Specifically, a whopping two-thirds of each chamber has to vote in favor of the amendment. There's another, less traveled path, though. If two-thirds of state legislatures decide they're not thrilled with Congress's pace (or lack thereof) on a certain issue, they can call for a convention to propose the amendment directly. This latter method sounds exciting but hasn't actually been used for any of our current amendments.

Once an amendment is proposed, the real hustle begins. It needs ratification, which is just a fancy way of saying official approval. Here, the states get their say. Three-fourths of state legislatures or conventions (depending on the method specified by Congress) must give the thumbs up. The choice between legislatures and conventions is interesting. Using state legislatures is pretty straightforward, but sometimes, for very hot-button issues, conventions can offer a direct line to the people's voice, minimizing political maneuvering. Regardless of the method, reaching this level of consensus is no small feat, making each successful amendment a true testament to its necessity and relevance.

The timeline for this ratification process can vary. Sometimes, Congress sets a deadline, creating a ticking clock scenario. This deadline adds a bit of drama to the process, emphasizing the need for swift action if the amendment is to succeed. If the deadline is missed, the amendment proposal basically goes into history's recycle bin, needing to start from scratch if it's ever to be considered again.

What's truly fascinating is how this process underscores the balance of power and the critical role of compromise in our democracy. Each step requires negotiation, reflection, and, ultimately, agreement on what values and principles are so fundamental that they deserve a permanent spot in the Constitution. So, whenever a new amendment makes its way through this gauntlet, it's a pretty big deal—an enduring change that reflects the will and evolution of the American people.

Chapter 8:
Future Amendments: What's Next?

As we peer into the future of the U.S. Constitution, it's like trying to guess the ending of a story that's still being written. What's clear, though, is that change is a part of the Constitution's DNA. It was created to evolve, to adapt to new ideas and societal shifts. Picture this: new amendments could emerge, addressing today's hot-button issues like digital privacy, climate change, or even the structure of our government itself. But, adding amendments isn't a walk in the park. It takes a powerful mix of public support, political will, and sometimes, a push from grassroots movements to get the ball rolling. Keeping in mind, the Constitution has only been amended 27 times since 1787, which shows just how high the bar is set. The process requires a hefty dose of compromise and consensus-building, reflecting the nation's diverse views and values. As we look ahead, it's anyone's guess which amendments will next find their way into this venerable document, but the journey there promises to be a test of our collective commitment to shaping a fair, just, and evolving society.

Potential Amendments and Movements

As we turn our gaze towards the horizon of American constitutional law, we find ourselves amidst a lively debate on what the next amendments might be. The Constitution, after all, isn't a static document. It's designed to evolve, to breathe fresh air into the lungs of democracy as times change. So what's next? Well, let's dive into some of the movements and potential amendments gaining traction today.

First off, there's a growing conversation about an Equal Rights Amendment (ERA). The idea isn't new—it's been around since the 1920s—but the push for gender equality under the Constitution has picked up steam recently. The ERA aims to guarantee equal legal rights for all American citizens regardless of sex. It's about making sure that gender equality isn't just a moral or social standard but a constitutional one.

Another hot topic is electoral reform. Some folks are advocating for an amendment to abolish the Electoral College, arguing it's outdated and doesn't reflect the true voice of the American people. Instead, they propose a system where the President is elected by a direct popular vote. The debate here is intense, with strong opinions on both sides.

Then there's the issue of campaign finance reform. In the aftermath of decisions like Citizens United, many are calling for a constitutional amendment to limit the influence of money in politics. The goal? To ensure that elections are a fair play, where the depth of one's pocket doesn't dictate the breadth of their political influence.

Privacy rights in the digital age are also sparking conversations. As technology advances, some argue that the Constitution needs an update to protect citizens' rights in the face of digital surveillance and data collection. This could mean an amendment that clearly defines the right to digital privacy, making sure our online lives are safeguarded by the Constitution.

Climate change, believe it or not, is another area where people are discussing constitutional amendments. With the growing urgency of the climate crisis, some activists propose an amendment that would compel the government to take decisive actions against environmental degradation. It's a bold move, aiming to engrain the fight against climate change into the nation's foundational laws.

On a different note, there's talk about an amendment to clarify the succession process for high government officials. While the 25th Amendment addresses presidential disability and succession, some suggest that recent events highlight the need for more detailed procedures. It's about ensuring the stability and continuity of government, no matter what happens.

Let's not forget the movement to secure voting rights more explicitly. Despite amendments aimed at extending the franchise, voting rights have been a contentious issue, with debates over voter ID laws, gerrymandering, and disenfranchisement. An amendment here would aim to protect and expand the right to vote, making it clear and unequivocal.

Of course, all these potential amendments face significant hurdles. Changing the Constitution is no easy feat. It requires broad consensus and, often, a push from a movement strong enough to sway both public opinion and the political landscape.

So, what does all this mean for you? It's simple. As citizens, we have a voice in shaping the future of our Constitution. Whether it's through advocating, voting, or simply staying informed, we play a part in the ongoing story of American democracy. The potential amendments and movements we see today are a reminder of our role in that process.

In closing, the Constitution isn't just a relic of the past. It's a living document, one that grows with us, reflecting our values, our struggles, and our progress. The discussion on future amendments is a testament to our enduring commitment to a more perfect union. And who knows? Maybe one of these potential amendments will be the next big chapter in our constitutional story.

Chapter 9:
Your Questions Answered

In the journey of unpacking the U.S. Constitution, we've touched on its amendments, cases, and real-world applications. Now, it's time to dial into what's buzzing in your mind. This chapter is all about demystifying the Constitution in the most straightforward way possible. Think of it as a casual chat over coffee, where no question is too simple or too complex. Are you wondering if there's a loophole in the Second Amendment, or why the 19th Amendment was such a game-changer? Maybe you're curious about how the 25th Amendment might work in real life? We've pooled together the most frequent head-scratchers and broken them down. The aim here isn't to overload you with jargon but to clear the air and provide clarity. Whether it's about your rights in a digital era, understanding how amendments can be made, or simply wanting to know more about the unsung heroes behind these historical changes, we've got you covered. Let's navigate through these curiosities together, ensuring that by the end of this chapter, the Constitution feels less like a distant relic and more like an everyday guide for all of us.

FAQs About the Constitution and Your Rights

So, you've been hearing a lot about the Constitution and wondering how it applies to you, right? Let's break it down into some frequently asked questions that might be bobbing around in your head. Our aim here is to make understanding this historic document a tad simpler, so you can see its impact on your daily life.

First up, **what rights do I have under the Constitution?** At its heart, the Constitution and especially the Bill of Rights lay out the liberties guaranteed to every American. We're talking freedom of speech, religion, the press, the right to assemble peacefully, and petition the government. There's also the right to keep and bear arms, protections against unreasonable searches and seizures, and rights concerning criminal and civil legal proceedings. Plus, there are amendments that have extended rights, like voting rights, across age, race, and gender.

Another common question is, **how does the Constitution protect these rights?** It's got a system of checks and balances spread across three branches of government—the Legislative, Executive, and Judicial—to ensure no single part gets too powerful. The courts, especially the Supreme Court, play a crucial role in interpreting the Constitution, making sure that laws and government actions comply with it. This way, your rights are protected from being infringed upon by the government.

Many also wonder, **can the Constitution change?** Absolutely. The framers made sure to include a process for amendments. This means the Constitution isn't frozen in time but can adapt with society. To date, there have been 27 amendments, showing that change is part of its strength.

What about my right to privacy? This one's interesting because the word "privacy" doesn't actually appear in the text. However, the Supreme Court has interpreted certain amendments, like the Fourth (protection against unreasonable searches and seizures), as providing a right to privacy. This has been expanded over the years to include decisions about personal life, such as marriage and childbearing.

Another hot topic: **what does the Second Amendment really allow?** The Second Amendment protects the right to keep and bear arms, but it's subject to ongoing debate and interpretation. The courts have supported reasonable regulations, like background checks and restrictions on certain types of firearms, to protect public safety while respecting individuals' rights to self-defense.

Then there's the question, **do states have rights too?** Yes, indeed. The Tenth Amendment clarifies that powers not delegated to the federal government are reserved to the states or to the people. This ensures a balance of power between state and federal governments, a setup known as federalism.

And what if you feel your rights have been violated? This is where it gets practical. You can seek redress through the judicial system. Courts can review whether your constitutional rights have been infringed upon and provide remedies. This might mean suing a government body or an official, or sometimes, defense in criminal proceedings.

Lastly, many are curious, **how can I make my voice heard?** Voting is your go-to tool here. Beyond that, engage with your representatives, participate in peaceful protests, petitions, and public forums. The First Amendment's got your back, ensuring you can speak up, assemble, and petition the government.

Understanding the Constitution isn't just academic; it's about knowing your rights and responsibilities in this tapestry of democracy. It empowers you to be an informed citizen, actively participating in shaping the society you live in. That's the essence of what it means to be part of this ongoing experiment in self-government.

Chapter 10:
The Constitution in Daily
Life: Case Studies

Let's talk real talk—how does something as grand as the Constitution influence your everyday life? You might not think about it much, but the rules and rights laid out in this historic document are quietly shaping the world around you. Through various case studies, this chapter peels back the layers on the Constitution's impact on daily life, showing not just how these principles apply in courtrooms and government offices but how they affect the little things, like the privacy of your home, the freedom to express yourself on social media, and even your trip through airport security. We've gathered stories from coast to coast, each one highlighting a moment where someone's day-to-day life intersected with constitutional principles. From the student who challenged her school dress code on the basis of free speech to the small business owner navigating the complexities of the Second Amendment, these real-life examples demonstrate the Constitution isn't just a relic of the past—it's a living, breathing part of our present. By exploring these case studies, you'll see the Constitution doesn't only exist in the high courts; it's at your family dinner table, on your social media feed, and in every aspect of your personal quest for life, liberty, and the pursuit of happiness.

Real-Life Examples of the Constitution at Work

When we talk about the Constitution, it's easy to picture a historic document under glass – something distant and maybe a bit abstract. But let's shift gears and see how it's anything but that. The Constitution is alive in the daily lives of Americans, influencing situations that range from the mundane to the monumental. Here are some real-life examples that show the Constitution isn't just a relic; it's a living, breathing guide to freedom and justice.

Imagine this: It's an election year, and the airwaves are buzzing. Candidates are everywhere, making their cases. Thanks to the First Amendment, they can express their views freely, and so can you. This freedom to speak our minds, debate, and campaign is foundational, allowing democracy to thrive. Whether you're voicing support, dissent, or questioning candidates on social media, the First Amendment protects your right to do so.

Now, let's talk guns. The Second Amendment guarantees the right to bear arms, a topic of heated debate. In rural areas, a family's tradition of hunting passes from generation to generation, all under the umbrella of constitutional protection. In urban communities, discussions about gun regulation and rights under the same amendment are robust and lively. This single sentence in our Constitution underpins a nationwide conversation about safety, rights, and freedom.

Consider a world where you're considered guilty until proven innocent, where your property can be searched without reason. Thankfully, the Fourth Amendment safeguards us against unreasonable searches and seizures, requiring law enforcement to have a warrant to enter our homes. This protection ensures our privacy is respected, reflecting the importance of individual rights at the core of the Constitution.

Now imagine you're called to serve as a juror, an experience many Americans have. The Sixth Amendment guarantees the accused in criminal prosecutions the right to a speedy and public trial by an impartial jury. Serving on a jury, you're directly participating in the justice system, upholding the Constitution's promise of fairness and protection under the law.

Ever noticed how the First Amendment also protects the freedom of religion? Across America, people attend churches, temples, mosques, and other places of worship freely. This diversity in belief and the harmony in which we generally practice signify the Constitution's powerful role in protecting our rights to believe as we choose, worship, or not worship at all.

Freedom of the press, another gem from the First Amendment, enables journalists to report, investigate, and critique the government without fear of reprisal. This freedom is a cornerstone of our democracy, empowering a free exchange of information and holding those in power accountable.

The Eighth Amendment's prohibition against cruel and unusual punishment ensures humane treatment within the criminal justice system. This principle guides everything from sentencing standards to prison conditions, reflecting the Constitution's commitment to dignity and justice for all, regardless of circumstance.

Then there's the matter of voting. The Fifteenth, Nineteenth, and Twenty-Sixth Amendments together have expanded voting rights across race, gender, and age. Every time you vote, you're participating in a process shaped by centuries of constitutional evolution aimed at making our democracy more inclusive.

The Thirteenth Amendment abolished slavery, a transformational moment in U.S. history. Its impact reverberates today in ongoing conversations about race, equality, and justice, underlining the

Constitution's role in shaping and reshaping our society's moral compass.

The Fourth Amendment's stand on privacy isn't just about searches and seizures; it's increasingly relevant in our digital lives. As we navigate the internet, the protections against unwarranted government intrusion ensure our digital spaces are extensions of our private lives, deserving of respect and protection.

The Seventh Amendment might seem less known, but its guarantee of a jury trial in civil cases is a key aspect of our legal system, ensuring that disputes between citizens can be resolved fairly, preserving the integrity of our justice system and the trust of those it serves.

What about the times when speech can cause harm or chaos? The First Amendment protects free speech, but it's not absolute. Cases where speech incites violence or shares false information that can harm are not protected. This balance between free expression and public safety is a delicate dance we navigate daily, reflecting the Constitution's flexible strength.

Consider the Constitution's role in the internet age. The First Amendment doesn't mention the internet, but its protections of speech, assembly, and the press are pivotal in the digital realm. Every blog post, tweet, or online rally falls under the umbrella of freedoms the Framers championed centuries ago.

The Twenty-Fourth Amendment eliminated the poll tax, knocking down economic barriers to voting. This change empowered more Americans to participate in our democracy, echoing the Constitution's evolving nature as we strive toward a more equitable society.

Last but not least, imagine the process of passing an amendment itself. The Constitution provides a way to change it, reflecting society's evolving values and needs. This ability to amend is perhaps its most remarkable feature, ensuring that the Constitution remains relevant and responsive to the American people.

Through these examples, it's clear the Constitution isn't just a historical document—it's a vital part of everyday life, influencing everything from our rights and freedoms to how we engage with each other and the government. It empowers us, protects us, and challenges us, making it as integral to the American story today as it was over two centuries ago.

Conclusion

As we wrap up our journey through the U.S. Constitution, it's clear that this document isn't just a piece of paper tucked away in some museum - it's a living, breathing foundation that shapes our daily lives. Each amendment we've explored, from the guarantees of freedom in the Bill of Rights to the more recent changes that refine and expand our liberties, forms a patchwork that protects the rights of every American. But here's the kicker: the Constitution isn't just the government's responsibility; it's everybody's business. Your role in this epic story? It's more significant than you might think. Whether by voting, staying informed, or even rallying for change, your actions breathe life into these pages. We've seen how amendments aren't just historical footnotes but active tools that address modern issues, ensuring that liberty and justice aren't just lofty ideals but realities for all. Remember, the Constitution is poised to evolve, and you're part of that evolution - contributing to a legacy that'll outlast us all. So let's carry forward the torch of democracy, not just as heirs to an incredible legacy but as architects of the future. After all, in a democracy this vibrant, staying on the sidelines isn't an option.

Your Role in the Living Constitution

So, we've taken quite the journey through the ins and outs of the U.S. Constitution, from its first ten amendments, the Bill of Rights, to the later ones that have shaped the modern era. But understanding these elements isn't just an academic exercise. It points to something much bigger—the living, breathing nature of the Constitution and, more

101

importantly, your role within it. The Constitution isn't just a relic to be admired from afar; it's a dynamic framework that requires your participation to truly function.

First off, it's crucial to recognize that this document impacts your daily life in more ways than you might think. Whether it's safeguarding your speech online, protecting you during a legal dispute, or ensuring your vote counts in an election, the Constitution is at work. But here's the kicker: it can only protect and serve us as well as we understand and engage with it. That's where you come in. By staying informed about your rights and the current debates surrounding them, you contribute to a more vibrant and resilient democracy.

Next, exercising your rights is a fundamental aspect of living in a constitutional democracy. It's not just about voting in elections, though that's certainly key. It's also about being an active participant in your community, questioning decisions that affect you and your neighbors, and holding those in power accountable. The framers of the Constitution envisioned a populace that was engaged and informed, and though the world has changed in countless ways since then, that vision remains as critical as ever.

Moreover, protecting and extending the Constitution requires vigilance. As society evolves, so too do the challenges we face. Issues like digital privacy, climate change, and social equity demand our attention and action. Your voice, whether expressed through voting, advocacy, or public discourse, helps steer the collective conversation and ensures that the Constitution remains a living document—one that meets the needs and rights of all citizens.

In closing, the Constitution is what we make of it. Its continued relevance and strength depend not on its venerability but on its vitality in our everyday lives. So, engage, question, and participate. Your role in the living Constitution isn't just as a beneficiary of its protections but as a guardian of its promise. Let's not take this responsibility lightly. After all, democracy, much like a garden, thrives with care, attention, and the collective effort of those it nourishes.

Glossary of Terms

Let's dive into some key terms that'll help you make sense of everything we've talked about so far. Think of this glossary as your handy guide to understanding the U.S. Constitution, its amendments, and how they apply to daily life. We're keeping it straightforward, so you won't need a law degree to get it.

Amendment

An **amendment** is a change or addition to the Constitution. It's the way we make sure the Constitution grows and evolves with our country.

Bill of Rights

The first ten amendments to the Constitution, known collectively as the **Bill of Rights**, were written to protect individual freedoms and rights from government interference.

Civil Cases

Civil cases are legal disputes between two or more parties (individuals, organizations, or government entities) over issues such as contracts, property, and personal injuries, where criminal charges aren't involved.

Electoral College

The **Electoral College** is a system used to elect the President and Vice President. It includes electors from each state who cast votes based on the popular vote within their state.

Equal Protection Clause

Part of the 14th Amendment, the **Equal Protection Clause** requires states to treat all individuals equally under the law, protecting against discrimination.

Executive Branch

The **Executive Branch** is one of three branches of government, headed by the President, responsible for enforcing laws.

Judicial Branch

The **Judicial Branch**, led by the Supreme Court, interprets laws to decide what they mean and whether they conform to the Constitution.

Legislative Branch

The **Legislative Branch** is the part of government that makes laws. In the U.S., it's made up of two parts: the House of Representatives and the Senate.

Preamble

The **Preamble** is the introduction to the Constitution. It outlines the purpose behind the document and the aspirations for the nation.

Ratification

Ratification is the official way to confirm something, usually by voting. The Constitution and its amendments became law once they were ratified by the states.

Self-Incrimination

The act of implicating oneself in a crime. The Fifth Amendment protects against **self-incrimination**, meaning you can't be forced to testify against yourself.

Separation of Powers

This principle divides the government into three branches (legislative, executive, judicial), each with its own powers and responsibilities to prevent any one branch from becoming too powerful.

And there you have it—a glossary of key terms to help guide you through the complexities of the U.S. Constitution. Keep this list handy as you continue exploring how the Constitution impacts your life and the lives of those around you.

Important Constitutional Documents

When we talk about the foundation of the United States, a few key documents come to mind. These aren't just pieces of paper tucked away in some museum; they are the backbone of American democracy, shaping the rights and freedoms we enjoy today. So, let's break them down into bite-sized pieces, making it easier to understand why they matter to you and me.

The Declaration of Independence - Think of this as America's break-up letter with Great Britain. Written in 1776, it's a bold statement declaring why the thirteen colonies deserved to be independent states, free from British rule. It's famous for its line about life, liberty, and the pursuit of happiness - ideals that still define the American dream.

The Constitution - This is the big one. Ratified in 1788, the Constitution lays out the entire framework of the U.S. government. It's like the rule book for how the country should run, detailing everything from the powers of the President to the rights of individual citizens. If the U.S. were a game, the Constitution would be the instructions everyone has to follow.

The Bill of Rights - These are the first ten amendments to the Constitution, added in 1791. They're a list of guarantees that protect some of our most fundamental rights, like freedom of speech, the right to a fair trial, and yes, the right to bear arms. These amendments assure that the government can't infringe on our personal freedoms.

The Federalist Papers - Not a single document but a collection of 85 essays written by Alexander Hamilton, James Madison, and John Jay. These writings played a huge role in getting the Constitution ratified. They're like a detailed FAQ for citizens of the late 1700s who had questions about how the new government would work.

The Articles of Confederation - This was America's first attempt at a constitution, ratified in 1781. It was more like a rough draft that didn't quite hit the mark, creating a weak national government that struggled to function. Think of it as the beta test for the U.S. government, leading to the major upgrade that was the Constitution.

Understanding these documents helps us see the bigger picture. They show us not just how the U.S. was formed but also the values it was founded upon. In our current age, where it's easy to take our rights for granted, revisiting these documents can remind us of the struggles and debates that shaped the nation. They're not just relics of the past but living pieces of history that continue to influence our lives today.

So next time you hear someone refer to the Constitution or the Bill of Rights, you'll know it's not just political jargon. These documents are assurances that your voice matters, your rights are protected, and you're part of something bigger – a democracy that's been evolving for over two centuries. And that's something worth understanding, and more importantly, worth protecting.

Knowing these documents, you're not just memorizing facts for a history test. You're arming yourself with knowledge about your own rights and freedoms. It's understanding the rulebook of the country, and that's powerful. So when discussions about constitutional rights pop up, you won't just be reciting what someone else said; you'll be speaking from a place of knowledge.

Now, don't worry if you can't remember every article or amendment right away. It's about getting familiar with the spirit of these documents. With time, and maybe a little patience, you'll start to see just how relevant the Constitution and its companions are to your daily life. They're not just a part of history classes; they're a vital part of American life, including yours.

So, as we move on, keep these documents in mind. They're the stars that guide the ship of state, the benchmarks for evaluating our laws, and the foundation of our rights and freedoms. By understanding them, you're taking a step toward being a more informed citizen, ready to contribute to the ongoing story of American democracy.

Further Reading/Resources

Getting your head around the Constitution and how it applies to our lives today can be a lot, but thankfully, there's a world of resources out there to help make these concepts bite-sized and digestible. If you've finished this book and you're craving more or perhaps looking for different perspectives, we've got you covered. First off, the classic, "The Federalist Papers," written by Alexander Hamilton, James Madison, and John Jay, is a fantastic deep dive into the minds of those who crafted the framework of the U.S. Constitution. It might not be a light read, but it's packed with insights and analysis that are as relevant today as they were back in 1788.

For those who prefer something a bit more contemporary, podcasts like "More Perfect" by RadioLab offer an engaging exploration of the Supreme Court's decisions and how they shape our society. Each episode unpacks a piece of constitutional law in a way that's both accessible and thought-provoking, perfect for commutes or quiet evenings at home. If you're more visually inclined, the series "Constitution USA with Peter Sagal" on PBS takes a road trip through the nation's constitution, blending history, interviews, and a touch of humor to illuminate the document's modern-day application.

If you're the kind who likes to have a book in hand, "The Words We Live By: Your Annotated Guide to the Constitution" by Linda R. Monk breaks down the dense language of the Constitution into plain English, offering explanations and historical context that bring the document to life. Additionally, visiting websites like the National Archives (archives.gov) can connect you directly with the original documents and a treasure trove of educational materials. Remember, these resources are just the beginning. The more you explore, the better you'll understand the living, breathing document that guides American life and the rights it guarantees each one of us.

How to Contact Your Representatives

Staying in touch with the folks who help make our laws is easier now than ever before. They're there to listen to what you've got to say because, well, that's a big part of their job. Whether it's an email, a phone call, or a letter, reaching out to your representatives lets them know what matters to you. Plus, it's a solid way to exercise your rights. Finding who represents you at the federal, state, and local levels can usually be as simple as a quick search on the internet. Each elected official will have contact information listed on their official website.

Now, when you're ready to make that call or send that email, keep a few things in mind. Be clear about what issue you're contacting them about. It helps to be informed about the topic, so you're both on the same page. Don't worry, you don't have to be an expert, but a little homework goes a long way. And remember, being respectful and concise can make a big difference in how your message is received.

They're used to getting a lot of communications, so making your point effectively and politely is key.

What if you want to go a step further? Town hall meetings, public forums, and even social media platforms are great ways to engage more directly. These settings offer a chance to ask questions, get answers, and see firsthand how representatives are speaking and acting on your behalf. Plus, it's a two-way street – they get to hear directly from you. Influencing change starts with a single step, and getting in touch with your representatives is a powerful way to make sure your voice is heard. So, don't hesitate. Pick up the phone, write that email, or attend that meeting. Your opinions and concerns matter, and they're waiting to hear from you.